THE M. & E. HANDBOOK SERIES

LAW FOR JOURNALISTS

D1794729

THE M. & E. HANDBOOK SERIES

LAW FOR JOURNALISTS

ANTHONY RICHARDS, LL.B.

of the Press Association Law Service;
Lecturer in Law at Barking College of Technology

MACDONALD AND EVANS

MACDONALD & EVANS LTD.
Estover, Plymouth PL6 7PZ

First published 1977

©
MACDONALD AND EVANS LIMITED
1977

ISBN: 0 7121 1240 5

*Printed in Great Britain by
Hazell Watson & Viney Ltd
Aylesbury, Bucks*

FOREWORD

IT was both pleasurable and instructive to read this new book by Mr. Anthony Richards. Although it is intended primarily for journalists it would do exceedingly well as pabulum for the aspiring law student. It has three great merits. It is concise. It is clear. It is up-to-date. How seldom, alas, can that be said of any legal textbook. So much is happening nowadays to the law, which, as the pundits remind us, is a living thing, that I feel that it will not be long before a second edition is called for.

I have not read the passage on the subject of copyright for the reason that this is a matter about which I know very little, and it follows that my opinion as to its merits or demerits would be of very little value.

With the remaining subjects with which the book concerns itself I have had a nodding acquaintance acquired in the forty-seven years since I was first called to the bar, and I have no hesitation in saying to an intending purchaser that however horrifying the price may be, as indeed in these terrible times it always is, Mr. Richards' work is well worth the money.

The Hon. Mr. Justice Faulks
Chairman of the Committee on Defamation

PREFACE

THIS book has been written to cater for the needs of trainees in the newspaper and allied fields, but I hope that it will prove a useful work of reference throughout the communications industry generally.

It covers the syllabuses of various courses for trainees, and gives examples of various ways in which journalists have fallen foul of the law (and numerous cases where they have emerged triumphant). The Table of Cases is included in order to enable anyone who is interested in particular cases, and has access to a law library, to pursue them further.

At a time when numerous rights of the citizen (and, with them, rights of journalists) are undergoing constant erosion, journalists should guard them jealously. I hope that a wider awareness of their rights will lead journalists vigorously to assert them when, for example, local authorities or courts seek to act in violation of them.

I am deeply indebted to The Hon. Mr. Justice Faulks for so kindly agreeing to write a foreword to this book. He is a man who, both at the Bar and on the Bench, has earned the universal affection and respect of journalists.

I am indebted to the following for permissions to reproduce extracts from other works: Sweet & Maxwell Ltd., Butterworth & Co. (Publishers) Ltd., Professor Harry Street, Penguin Books Ltd., *Cambridge Law Journal*, *The Times*, *The Observer*, and the Law Commission.

I wish to thank the Press Association for permission to use its news library for research for this book; the staff of that library, and of the Middle Temple Library and the British Museum Newspaper Library; and colleagues and friends on the Press Association Law Service, in the Middle Temple, and in King's College, University of London.

I am also grateful to the publishers, and in particular to Mr. Pat Turtle for his untiring efforts and helpful advice in editing this book.

Any errors or omissions are, however, mine.

I have endeavoured to state the law as at 1st January 1977.

January 1977   ANTHONY J. RICHARDS

NOTICE TO LECTURERS

CONTENTS

TABLE OF CASES

CHAPTER I

LIBEL—DEFAMATORY STATEMENTS

WHAT IS DEFAMATORY?

1. Explanation. The law of libel exists to provide a remedy for wrongful injury to a person's reputation.

2. Civil and criminal libel. A libel may be both a tort (a civil wrong giving rise to a cause of action for damages) and a crime (giving rise to a criminal penalty). As a tort it consists of the wrongful publication of a defamatory statement. As a crime it consists of the publication of words calculated to provoke a breach of the peace (*see* V, **1**). Proceedings for criminal libel are rare. Except for Chapter V, **1**, Chapters I to V are concerned exclusively with civil libel.

3. Meaning of "defamatory statement". A defamatory statement is one which lowers a person "in the estimation of right-thinking members of society generally" (Lord Atkin in *Sim* v. *Stretch* (1936)); or "exposes him to hatred, contempt or ridicule" (Baron Parke in *Parmiter* v. *Coupland* (1840)); or injures him in his business or employment (Lord Blackburn in *Capital & Counties Bank* v. *Henty* (1882)); or causes others to shun him (*Bloodworth* v. *Gray* (1844)).

The Faulks Committee on Defamation recommended in 1975 the definition: "Matter which in all the circumstances would be likely to affect a person adversely in the estimation of reasonable people generally".

NOTE: a defamatory statement on radio or television is libel, not slander—*Defamation Act* 1952, *s*. 1.

4. "Right-thinking persons". A statement is not defamatory if right-thinking persons in society would not so regard it. Thus to say of an Irish priest that he would betray to the police "men who are ready to give up all for Ireland" (a "tout" in modern I.R.A. parlance) is not defamatory (*Mawe* v. *Pigott*

1

(1869)); neither is an allegation that a golf club member told police of an illegal gaming machine on club premises (*Byrne* v. *Deane* (1937)).

In *Mycroft* v. *Sleight* (1921) a judge said an allegation that a trade unionist had attempted to work during a strike would be defamatory because it would be so regarded, not only by his fellow trade unionists, but by "ordinary, just and reasonable citizens" generally.

5. Kinds of imputation. The categories of imputation which can give rise to a libel are never closed. The list is inexhaustible, but the following paragraphs give some common examples.

6. Imputations of dishonest or dishonourable conduct. Examples: cheating at brag (*Paterson* v. *Shaw* (1830)); cowardice (*Randolph Churchill* v. *Sir Gerald Nabarro* (1960)); ingratitude (*Cox* v. *Lee* (1869)); bad sportsmanship (*Lloyd* v. *Hickley* (1967)); maltreating employees (*Le Fanu* v. *Malcolmson* (1848)).

7. Imputations of unfitness for office. "Words which impute misconduct in an office, profession, trade or business" are defamatory (*Foulger* v. *Newcomb* (1867)). Examples:

(*a*) allegation that a doctor's lack of care had caused patients' deaths (*Southee* v. *Denny* (1847));

(*b*) allegation that a journalist was reckless (*Tracy* v. *Kemsley Newspapers Ltd.* (1954)).

(*c*) allegation that an election candidate "promises a lot, but never does anything" (*Pratten* v. *Labour Daily* (1926));

(*d*) allegation that an architect was incompetent (*Botterill* v. *Whytehead* (1879)).

8. Imputations of immorality. In *Liberace* v. *Daily Mirror Newspapers Ltd.* (1959), the newspaper described Liberace as "the pinnacle of masculine, feminine and neuter". The jury found an imputation of homosexuality, and that it was defamatory. A similar imputation is possible in the use of the word "pansies" (*Thaarup* v. *Hulton Press Ltd.* (1943)).

Mistakes over marriages or marriage dates can be libellous: e.g. a statement that a woman's marriage was a month before her child's birth (*Morrison* v. *Ritchie* (1902)); or that an unmarried actress had a child (*Chattell* v. *Daily Mail* (1901)); and *see Cassidy* v. *Daily Mirror Newspapers*, **20** below.

A mix-up over photographs, resulting in the wrong man's picture being published as that of an accused man in a vice trial, has proved to be a costly mistake (*Smith-Bingham* v. *Press Association Ltd.* (1975)).

9. Imputations of financial embarrassment. There is no shame in being poor; but an imputation of financial difficulties may affect the borrowing capacity of a person or trading concern, and cause creditors to close in. Examples:

(*a*) allegation that plaintiff had had to borrow to pay his rent (*Eaton* v. *Johns* (1842));

(*b*) mis-statement that plaintiff's bank account had insufficient funds to meet a cheque (*Davidson* v. *Barclay's Bank Ltd.* (1940)).

In *Capital & Counties Bank* v. *Henty* (1882) a statement that a large company was refusing to accept cheques drawn on the plaintiff bank was held not capable of meaning to ordinary men that the bank was insolvent. The decision was criticised by Lord Justice Salmon in *Slim* v. *Daily Telegraph* (1968): ". . . [the words] caused a run on the bank, whose customers were, presumably, ordinary men".

10. Imputations of illness. There is no shame in being ill; but an imputation that a person is suffering from a physical or mental disability may affect his prospects of employment or promotion.

Allegations that a person is suffering from a contagious disease (*Bloodworth* v. *Gray* (1844)) or has had a mental breakdown (*Bower* v. *Sunday Pictorial Newspapers Ltd.* (1962)) have been held defamatory.

11. Words causing ridicule. In *Cook* v. *Ward* (1830), Cook sued successfully over a "ludicrous" story that he had been mistaken for a hangman.

Ridicule arising from the following has been held not defamatory:

(*a*) the statement that a stockbroker liked playing with a yo-yo (*Blennerhasset* v. *Novelty Sales Co.* (1933));

(*b*) the report of a wedding the day before the event, thereby subjecting the bridegroom to "ridicule" from workmates (*Emerson* v. *Grimsby Times Co. Ltd.* (1926)).

WHO IS DEFAMED?

12. Even a criminal has a good name. Few people are so notorious as to enable journalists to vilify them with impunity. A criminal with a long history of burglary would no doubt swiftly sue if it were wrongly suggested that he had also been convicted of a sexual offence.

In *Bower* v. *Sunday Pictorial Newspapers Ltd.* (1962), where the plaintiff was serving a sentence for attempted murder, the jury rejected the argument that his crime had almost totally destroyed his repute, and that an allegation of mental breakdown therefore did him no harm.

Where, however, the words do the plaintiff no substantial harm, and the court considers the action ought never to have been brought, contemptuous damages will be awarded (*see* IV, **5**).

13. Words must refer to plaintiff. The words must be capable, in the mind of a reasonable person, of referring to the plaintiff. They need not necessarily name him: e.g. in *J'Anson* v. *Stuart* (1787), where a man was described as "having but one eye" and a name like that of "a certain noble circumnavigator", the words were held to refer to the plaintiff.

A reference to a person by name only, with no other identifying particulars (*see Newstead* v. *London Express Newspapers Ltd.*, II, **12** and **35**) may be taken to "refer" to a namesake.

14. Generally no libel of a group. "If a man wrote that all lawyers were thieves, no particular lawyer could sue him unless there is something to point to that particular individual" (Mr. Justice Willes in *Eastwood* v. *Holmes* (1858)).

The *Daily Express* alleged that a "minute body" in wartime Britain was Fascist. The plaintiff, a member of that group, sued unsuccessfully for damages for libel. He was not singled out. (*Knupffer* v. *London Express Newspapers Ltd.* (1944)).

Contrast: *Le Fanu* v. *Malcolmson* (1848). A newspaper alleged cruelty to workers "in some of the Irish factories". A factory owner successfully sued, because other words in the story could be taken to refer to his factory in particular. Lord Campbell said that if the public knew at whom an allegation was aimed, it was "as if his name and Christian name were ten times repeated".

Where the group is small (e.g. a board of directors) each

member may sue. Where a magazine referred to Old Bailey journalists as "beer-sodden hacks", individual journalists there successfully sued for libel (*Glenton* v. *The Spectator* (1974)).

15. Libel of a public body. In *Bognor Regis U.D.C.* v. *Campion* (1972), damages were awarded over an allegation of "Toy Town Hitlerism" in a local authority. The judge distinguished the decision in *Manchester Corporation* v. *Williams* (1891) (that a public body, as such, could not be libelled) by saying that local authorities today relied on their reputations to fulfil their greatly extended functions, and could protect their reputations in the courts.

The *Campion* decision has been attacked (Weir, *Cambridge Law Journal*, 1972) as "in effect a gross invasion of civil liberties, and in method a serious reproach to English law".

It is well established that companies (*D. & L. Caterers Ltd.* v. *D'Anjou* (1945)) and trade unions (*N.U.G.M.W.* v. *Gillian* (1946)) can sue for libel.

16. No libel of the dead. Defamatory words about a deceased person will not give surviving relatives a cause of action unless the words also reflect on them; but they could give rise to prosecution for criminal libel (*see* V, **1**).

Where either party to a libel suit dies before the action is disposed of, it dies with him. The Faulks Committee recommended that close relatives of a deceased person should be able to sue for defamation of him within five years of his death, but should not be entitled to damages, only to a declaration that the words are untrue, and an injunction against their repetition. The Committee also recommended that, where a defamation action has been started before a party's death, it should survive for the benefit of, or against, his estate.

INTERPRETATION OF WORDS

17. Natural meaning. "Norma loquendi" [everyday speech] is the rule for the interpretation of words, and "words which an hundred years ago would not import a slanderous sense may now". (*Harrison* v. *Thornborough* (1714)). To have called a person "gay" twenty years ago would not have been defamatory; today it may well be so.

In *Lewis* v. *Daily Telegraph* (1964), Lord Reid said the

"ordinary man" does not live in an ivory tower, and "reads between the lines" in the light of his worldly experience.

In *Barnett* v. *Allen* (1858), the plaintiff contended that "blackleg" (in those days) meant a dishonest gambler. Two judges agreed. The case shows how meanings of words change over the years.

In 1959, the pianist Liberace sued Daily Mirror Newspapers Ltd. over his description as ". . . everything that he, she or it can ever want . . . [a] sniggering, snuggling, chromium-plated, scent-impregnated . . . ice-covered heap of mother-love". No innuendo (*see* 20) was pleaded, but the jury found that, on their *natural* meaning, the words imputed homosexuality.

A newspaper advertisement that "the public are informed that [X's] connection with the Walsall Scientific Institute has ceased, and he is not authorised to receive subscriptions on its behalf", has been held not capable of a defamatory meaning (*Mulligan* v. *Cole* (1875)). The decision is questionable; the obvious meaning was that, if the public were not warned, the plaintiff might pocket monies to which he was not entitled.

A statement that a company would not accept cheques drawn on a certain bank has been held not capable of meaning that the bank was insolvent (*Capital & Counties Bank* v. *Henty* (1882)—but *see* the criticism in 9).

18. Proof of meaning. The onus is on the plaintiff to establish the meaning for which he contends. He will fail if no reasonable reader would read the article as bearing the meaning alleged—*Astaire* v. *Campling* (1966).

In deciding whether the words are capable of bearing the meaning alleged (this is a function of the judge, not the jury— *see* IV, 2) "mere conjectures" which a reader might form should not be taken into account—Lord Selborne in the *Capital & Counties Bank* case.

19. Where two meanings are possible. "It seems to me unreasonable that, when there are a number of good interpretations, the only bad one should be seized upon to give a defamatory sense" to the statement—Lord Atkin in *Sim* v. *Stretch* (1936).

But where two or more meanings would be equally likely to be conveyed to a reasonable reader, the judge should leave the question for the jury (*Stubbs* v. *Russell* (1913)).

In *Thaarup* v. *Hulton Press Ltd.* (1943), Lord Justice Scott said it was a question for the jury whether words in *Lilliput*— "I only wanted a few pansies"—bore an innocent or sinister meaning.

20. Innuendo. A seemingly innocuous statement may contain a hidden defamatory meaning.

Examples:

The *Daily Mirror* published a photograph of a Mr. Cassidy and Miss X, with a caption that they intended marriage. Cassidy was already married. HELD: his wife had been libelled, because the caption implied that Cassidy was free to marry, and led some of his wife's friends to think that she and he must therefore have been co-habiting outside wedlock (*Cassidy* v. *Daily Mirror Newspapers Ltd.* (1929)).

An advertisement for chocolate depicted, without his consent, a famous amateur golfer. HELD: libellous, the innuendo being that he had prostituted his amateur status by appearing in advertisements (*Tolley* v. *J. S. Fry & Sons Ltd.* (1931)).

The *Sun* stated that Miss A. had been kidnapped. She had shortly before been seen with a friend, Mr. Morgan. HELD: the article was not, in itself, capable of implying that Mr. Morgan kidnapped her, but (said Lord Reid) it was artificial to suggest that the identification of Mr. Morgan must be found in the words themselves, and not in extraneous circumstances. And, held the Law Lords, evidence may be admitted to give the words a defamatory meaning which they otherwise would not have had (*Morgan* v. *Odhams Press Ltd.* (1971)).

21. Libel by juxtaposition. A libel may consist of the publication of, e.g., a person's picture beside a wholly unconnected salacious story. In *Monson* v. *Tussauds* (1894) it was held potentially libellous to place a man's wax effigy beside those of murderers!

PROGRESS TEST 1

1. Distinguish between civil and criminal libel. **(2)**
2. Explain the meaning of "defamatory statement". **(3)**
3. What kinds of imputations commonly give rise to libel actions? **(5)**
4. Must a defamatory statement name the plaintiff? **(13)**

5. Is it libellous to write that "all journalists are drunkards"? **(14)**

6. Is it possible to libel (*a*) the dead, and (*b*) a public body? **(15, 16)**

7. Give examples of innuendos. **(20)**

CHAPTER II

LIBEL—DEFENCES

DEFENCES—GENERALLY

1. Civil libel defences. A defendant may plead justification, fair comment on a matter of public interest, privilege (absolute or qualified) or the defence of innocent defamation under *s.* 4, *Defamation Act* 1952. It is also possible, though rare, to adopt the apology procedure under the *Libel Act* 1843.

2. Relevance of intent and malice. It is no defence to show that the defamation was unintentional (unless it was also attended by reasonable care—*see* **34–8**). Malice will destroy the defences of fair comment and qualified privilege, but not absolute privilege or justification—except where the *Rehabilitation of Offenders Act* 1974 applies.

JUSTIFICATION

3. Explanation. The law does not inhibit, by civil libel, the publication of the truth (but a statement, though true, may nevertheless be, e.g., a breach of privilege, contempt of court, etc.; and see the qualifications in Chapter III). In *Sutherland* v. *Stopes* (1925) it was held that once the jury found that the words complained of were true, that disposed of the case. They did not need to consider a defence of fair comment.

4. Burden and standard of proof. A defendant who pleads justification must prove it. If he fails, the plea itself may exacerbate the damages. The standard of proof is the balance of probabilities—but, as Lord Denning has warned, "as the charge is grave, so the proof must be clear".

5. Full "sting" must be proved. A defendant must prove the full "sting" of his allegation. Example:

A newspaper alleged X had "bolted" from the neighbourhood, leaving debts unpaid. In fact he had departed leaving unpaid debts, but had not "bolted". X succeeded in a libel action, the imputation being that he had attempted to evade creditors (*O'Brien* v. *Bryant* 1846)).

6. One conviction does not make a "thief". An imputation of general bad character cannot be justified by one lapse. Examples:

A solicitor was rebuked by a court for his conduct of a case. A newspaper headlined the story: "How lawyer Bishop treats his clients". A plea of justification failed, because the words implied a *habitual* neglect of clients' affairs (*Bishop* v. *Latimer* (1861)).

A newspaper called a rival editor a "libellous journalist". HELD: one successful libel action again him did not justify this description (*Wakeley* v. *Cooke* (1849)).

7. Conviction is conclusive evidence. Douglas Goody and Alfred Hinds each recovered libel damages (Goody's were only nominal) over newspaper stories which stated that each had in fact committed a crime of which he had been convicted (*Goody* v. *Odhams Press Ltd.* (1967); *Hinds* v. *Sparkes* (1964)). This absurdity was cured by *s.* 13, *Civil Evidence Act* 1968:

". . . proof that, at the date when the issue falls to be determined, that person stands convicted of that offence, shall be conclusive evidence that he committed that offence; and his conviction thereof shall be admissible in evidence accordingly".

This section must now be read in the light of *ss.* 4(1) and 8, *Rehabilitation of Offenders Act* 1974 (*see* III, **1, 2**).

8. Reports and rumours. In the absence of privilege (*see* **10**) it is no defence to show that the words complained of were a report, however fair and accurate, of another person's defamatory statement. "If you report a rumour, you cannot say it is true by proving that the rumour existed. You have to prove that the subject matter of the rumour was true"—Lord Justice Greer in *Chapman* v. *Ellesmere* (1932).

9. Harmless inaccuracies immaterial. If the defendant proves the full sting of the allegation, his defence will not fail through some harmless inaccuracy. Example:

A report that a railway passenger had been fined £9, with an alternative of three weeks' imprisonment, for non-payment of his fare, was not deprived of the defence merely because the prison alternative was only two weeks (*Alexander* v. *N.E. Railway* (1865)).

The *Defamation Act* 1952, *s.* 5, now provides:

". . . a defence of justification shall not fail by reason only that the truth of every charge is not proved, if the words not proved to be true do not materially injure the plaintiff's reputation having regard to the truth of the remaining charges".

PRIVILEGE

10. Explanation. Privilege is a doctrine whereby the publisher of words is protected from suit for libel even though he cannot prove their truth. Privilege is of two kinds: absolute and qualified. Absolute privilege, so far as journalists are concerned, applies irrespective of any malice in the publication. Qualified privilege applies only if the words are published without malice. In either case the words must constitute a fair and accurate report.

11. Absolute privilege. The *Law of Libel Amendment Act* 1888, *s.* 3:

"A fair and accurate report in any newspaper of proceedings publicly heard before any court exercising judicial authority shall, if published contemporaneously with such proceedings, be privileged. Provided that nothing in this section shall authorise the publication of any blasphemous or indecent matter".

Although the word "absolute" does not appear in the section, it has been accepted as such in *Farmer* v. *Hyde* (1937) and by leading textbook writers.

NOTE: The *Defamation Act* 1952, *s.* 9, extends this defence to broadcasting; *s.* 8 restricts it to courts in the U.K.

12. "Fair and accurate report". Examples of how the privilege has been lost:

A report of evidence that "Constable Lee" had accepted a bribe described him as "Detective Lee". Two other officers of that name were in the force (*Lee and Lee* v. *Wilson* (1934)).

X was convicted of driving a car without consent, a charge of stealing it having been withdrawn. A newspaper reported the conviction as theft (*Mitchell* v. *Hirst, Kidd & Rennie* (1936)).

A newspaper reported evidence of a company's insolvency, omitting evidence in rebuttal which gave "an entirely different complexion" (*Wright & Greig* v. *Outram & Co.* (1890)).

A newspaper omitted X's denial of a murder charge, on which he was later acquitted (*Mitchell* v. *Victoria Daily Times* (1944)).

Evidence, instead of being attributed to the witness, was stated as a fact (*Grech* v. *Odhams Press Ltd.* (1958)).

A slight inaccuracy will not destroy the privilege, if the report as a whole is substantially accurate. Mr. Justice Byles in *Turner* v. *Sullivan* (1862): "Unless a fair and reasonable latitude were given, there would be no safety in reporting the proceedings in courts of justice."

However, even a fair and accurate report may be libellous if, through lack of particularity, it casts aspersions on a namesake. The *Daily Express*, reporting that "Harold Newstead, a Camberwell man" had been convicted of bigamy, omitted his age, occupation and address. A second Harold Newstead, living elsewhere in Camberwell, was held to have a cause of action for libel (*Newstead* v. *London Express Newspapers Ltd*, (1940)).

13. "In any newspaper". "Newspaper" for this purpose means "any paper containing public news, intelligence or occurrences, or any remarks or observations therein printed for sale, and published in England [and Wales] or Ireland periodically, or in parts or numbers at intervals not exceeding 26 days . . ." (*Newspaper Libel and Registration Act* 1881, *s.* 1).

14. "Proceedings".

(*a*) *Commencement and end.* An application before magistrates for a summons is a "proceeding", though heard in the other party's absence (*Kimber* v. *Press Association* (1893)). "Proceedings" continue until the court rises; thus remarks by a judge, after conclusion of a case but before rising, are part of "the proceedings" (*Glick* v. *Hinchcliffe* (1967)).

(*b*) *Unauthorised interruptions.* In *Hope* v. *Leng* (1907) a witness who had given evidence shouted "Lies" during subsequent evidence. It was held that the interruption was part of the "proceedings". being "a comment made by him when he was still under the obligation of the oath". The same ruling was applied in *Farmer* v. *Hyde* (1937), where the interrupter was the defendant—even though at that stage he had not been sworn. The position is likely to be different where the interrupter is a total stranger, e.g. :

> A stranger in the public gallery shouted that a witness's evidence was "nothing short of perjury". HELD: no privilege (*Lynam* v. *Gowring* (1880)).

(*c*) *Court documents.* Information contained in court documents, e.g. pleadings, affidavits, does not become privileged unless it is read out. In *Harper* v. *Provincial Newspapers Ltd.* (1937), a judge said that if false information, e.g. an address, were taken from a document which was "a mere exhibit in the case", it would not be privileged. The same applies to information from a charge sheet (*Furniss* v. *Cambridge Daily News Ltd.* (1907)).

(*d*) *Dress and demeanour.* A person's dress and demeanour in court are not part of "the proceedings".

15. "Publicly heard". Reports of proceedings heard in private do not have "the privilege which protects a full and fair report of proceedings in public open courts of justice"—Lord Atkinson in *Scott* v. *Scott* (1913).

16. "Court exercising judicial authority". It is submitted, in the absence of clear authority, that this extends to any court before which witnesses may be subpoenaed. In *McCarey* v. *Associated Newspapers* (1965) a coroner's court was held to be within the provision.

In *Albutt* v. *General Medical Council* (1889) it was suggested that a report of the Council's findings was "in the same position as a judicial report", but this was not a case under *s.* 3 (*see* **11** above).

17. "Published contemporaneously". There is no precise definition of "contemporaneous" for this purpose. *Gatley on Libel and Slander*, 7th Edn., submits that it means "as nearly at the same time as the proceedings as is reasonably possible, having regard to the opportunities for preparation of the report and the time of going to press or of making the broadcast".

The *Criminal Justice Act* 1967 provides that where publication of a report of committal proceedings is deferred to comply with *s*. 3(3) of that Act, the report will still be "contemporaneous" if published as soon as reasonably practicable after it becomes lawful to do so.

18. Rehabilitation of Offenders Act 1974. A report cannot be relied upon as a fair and accurate report if it includes evidence ruled to be inadmissible under this Act (*see* III, 2).

19. Qualified privilege. For this defence to succeed, the report must not only be fair and accurate, but must have been published bona fide and without malice. Examples follow below.

20. Parliamentary proceedings and papers. "A faithful newspaper report of a debate in either House of Parliament . . . will not give a right of action against the newspaper proprietor" (*Wason* v. *Walter* (1868)). This applies also to a verbal "sketch" of a Parliamentary debate (*Cook* v. *Alexander* (1974)).

The *Parliamentary Papers Act* 1840, *s*. 3, gives privilege for publication without malice of material from any report, paper, etc., published by order of either House. This includes a report presented *to* the House (*Mangena* v. *Lloyd* (1908)). But to embellish such a report with extraneous matter may destroy the privilege (*Dingle* v. *Associated Newspapers Ltd.* (1964)).

21. Defamation Act 1952, s. 7. This gives qualified privilege to certain reports—in some cases, with no requirement that the publisher shall, on request, publish an explanation or contradiction. In other cases, the privilege is subject to this requirement.

NOTE: "newspaper" here means one published at intervals not exceeding 36 days.

22. Reports requiring no explanation. These are fair and accurate reports of public proceedings of legislatures outside Britain, of an international organisation of which the U.K. is a member, or an international conference to which it sends a delegate, of an international court, of any court, public body or public inquiry in any part of H.M. Dominions outside the U.K., or of a British court martial outside the U.K.; a fair and accurate extract from a register which the British public is entitled to inspect; or a notice published on the authority of any court in the U.K.

NOTE: as to reports of foreign court proceedings, Mr. Justice Pearson suggested in *Webb* v. *Times Publishing Co. Ltd.* (1960) that a privilege applied so long as the English public interest in the foreign proceedings was a "legitimate and proper one", not based on "idle curiosity or a desire for gossip".

23. Reports requiring explanation. These are reports of:

(*a*) the findings or decision of any association formed in the U.K. to promote art, science, religion, learning, or any trade, business, industry or profession, or any game, sport or past-time, if the proceedings relate to a person subject to the association's jurisdiction;

(*b*) proceedings at any public meeting in the U.K. to discuss any matter of public concern, whether admission is restricted or not;

(*c*) fair and accurate reports of proceedings—in public—of local authorities or their committees, magistrates sitting otherwise than as a court, an inquiry commission, tribunal, etc., appointed by statute or by the Crown, a person appointed by a local authority to hold a local inquiry under any statute, or any other body exercising statutory functions;

(*d*) proceedings at a general meeting of a public company;

(*e*) a notice issued for public information by any government department, local authority or police.

24. Malice. The defence of qualified privilege will fail if the plaintiff proves that the publication was actuated by malice. "Malice" is not only spite or ill-will, but includes (per the Faulks Committee report) the taking of some improper advantage of the privileged occasion.

FAIR COMMENT

25. Explanation. A person may comment freely on matters of public interest, provided he does so without malice and without imputing improper motives to those whom he criticises.

26. Malice. A defence of fair comment will fail if the plaintiff proves malice (*see* **24**). Malice by an outside contributor (e.g.

the writer of a "letter to the editor") will not "infect" a bona fide publisher or editor (*Egger* v. *Viscount Chelmsford* (1964)). Nor will the fact that the writer's name and address turn out to be fictitious (*Lyon* v. *Daily Telegraph* (1943)).

27. Comment must be comment. "Comment, in order to be justifiable as fair comment, must appear as comment, and not to be so mixed up with facts that the reader cannot distinguish between what is report and what is comment"— Lord Justice Fletcher-Moulton in *Hunt* v. *Star Newspaper Co. Ltd.* (1908).

Thus the defence has failed where the allegation was that the artists in a play, who had simultaneously resigned from it, had "conspired" to close it down. The allegation of conspiracy was one of fact, not comment (*London Artists Ltd.* v. *Littler* (1969)).

28. Facts must be true or privileged. The comment must be based on facts which are true or, if untrue, privileged—e.g. taken from a judge's judgment, or a jury's verdict, or even from evidence (*Grech* v. *Odhams Press Ltd.* (1958)).

But the *Defamation Act* 1952, *s.* 6, provides:

> "In an action for libel . . . in respect of words consisting partly of allegations of fact and partly of expressions of opinion, a defence of fair comment shall not fail by reason only that every allegation of fact is not proved, if the expression of opinion is fair comment having regard to such of the facts alleged or referred to in the words complained of as are proved."

29. Facts must appear. The facts need not be expressly set out in the comment if they can be gleaned from it. "The question in all cases is whether there is a sufficient substratum of fact stated *or indicated* in the words which are the subject matter of the action." (Lord Porter in *Kemsley* v. *Foot* (1952)).

30. Facts must be known to commentator. The comment must be based on facts known to the maker. The *Daily Telegraph*, which commented on the "sad state" of a company, was unable, in a defence of fair comment, to rely on a *subsequent* resolution for the company's liquidation. Lord Denning said: "A man may comment on existing facts without having them all in the forefront of his mind. Nevertheless, it must be a comment on existing facts." (*Cohen* v. *Daily Telegraph Ltd.* (1968)).

31. Comment may be stinging. The severity of a comment will not destroy the defence if the opinion is honestly held and expressed without malice; but the use of immoderate language may provide some evidence of malice.

The *Sunday Express* made stinging comments about Lord Silkin's chairmanship of a company marketing German cars in Britain. Mr. Justice Diplock enunciated the test: that the opinion expressed, "however exaggerated, obstinate or prejudiced it may be", must have been honestly held by the writer. He directed the jury: "If you were to take the view that this was so strong a comment that no fair-minded man could honestly have expressed it, the defence fails." The defence succeeded (*Silkin* v. *Beaverbrook Newspapers Ltd.* (1958)).

A newspaper commented that a play was "composed of nothing but nonsense of a not very humorous character". The defence succeeded (*McQuire* v. *Western Morning News Ltd.* (1903)).

A newspaper described X, who had been convicted of rape, as a "vicious pest" who had given his victim a "night of terror". The defence succeeded. Mr. Justice Melford Stevenson said: "It would be a sad day if newspapers were forbidden to publish, and comment on, matters of public interest and facts leading to important convictions. They are entitled to comment provided they do so fairly and without malice." (*Levene* v. *News of the World Ltd.* (1972)).

32. Court's view irrelevant. It is irrelevant whether the court agrees with the opinion. "The jury might not agree with the opinions expressed, but they have no right to substitute their own opinions . . . or to try the fairness of the comments by this standard"—Lord Morton in *Turner* v. *M.G.M.* (1950).

33. "Public interest". The matter commented upon must be one in which the public are entitled to be interested. Examples:

(*a*) *Public figures.* Moral indiscretions of members of the government are arguably matters of public interest in that they reflect on the members' suitability for high office, and could expose them to blackmail. Similar conduct by persons outside public life would not be of public interest.

A newspaper said of a Q.C., who was also an M.P., that it

was extraordinary that he should be elevated to judicial office at a time when he was being arraigned before the Benchers of his Inn. The defence succeeded. His conduct, *if it had reference to his fitness to occupy a public position,* was a fair subject of debate (*Seymour* v. *Butterworth* (1862)).

(*b*) *Administration of justice.* Justice "must be allowed to suffer the outspoken, though respectful, comments of ordinary men"—Lord Atkin in *Ambard* v. *Attorney-General of Trinidad* (1936).

(*c*) *Central and local government.* "Whatever is a matter of public concern when administered in one of the government departments is a matter of public concern when administered by sub-ordinate authorities"—Chief Justice Cockburn in *Purcell* v. *Sowler* (1877).

Any matter involving the spending of public money, or the provision of services to the public, is one of public interest. Examples: the supply of gas (*Hedley* v. *Barlow* (1865)); vehicular use of a public right of way (*Slim* v. *Daily Telegraph Ltd.* (1968)); the construction of naval ships (*Henwood* v. *Harrison* (1872)); the administration of a workhouse (*Purcell* v. *Sowler* (1877).

(*d*) *Public performances.* Performances at places of public entertainment, e.g. theatres (*McQuire* v. *Western Morning News* (1903)), cinemas (*Turner* v. *M.G.M.* (1950), sporting events, are all matters of public interest.

This applies even if the promoters do not invite critics. In *Turner* v. *M.G.M.* Lord Morton said the film company could, if it wished, refrain from inviting a critic to a premiere, and the critic was "entitled, if she chose, to see their films in the same way as any other member of the public, and to comment on them . . ."

The same principles apply to reviews of literary, artistic, etc., works.

(*e*) *Other activities.* The conduct of trade unions or employers can have obvious repercussions on the community. The running of, e.g., public companies, newspapers (*Kemsley* v. *Foot* (1952)), or charities, are likewise legitimate objects of public concern.

Anyone embarking on an enterprise which is likely to affect others e.g. seeking planning permission which, if granted, is likely to change the face of a district) exposes himself to public criticism. A person who brings any matter into the limelight (e.g. by writing an open letter to a newspaper) must expect to himself become the target of criticism. "Critics are not exempt from criticism"—Lord Porter in *Turner* v. *M.G.M.*

UNINTENTIONAL DEFAMATION

34. Explanation. The *Defamation Act* 1952, *s.* 4, provides a special defence where words which are defamatory of another person are published innocently.

35. Meaning of "innocent publication". Words are published "innocently" only if all reasonable care was exercised in relation to their publication and either (*a*) the publisher knew of no circumstances whereby the words might refer to the plaintiff, or (*b*) the words were not defamatory on the face of them, and the publisher did not know of circumstances whereby they might be understood to be defamatory of the plaintiff.

The defence is unlikely to succeed in cases like *Hulton* v. *Jones* (1910) or *Newstead* v. *London Express Newspapers Ltd.* (1940), where characters in fiction or in newspaper stories have had real-life namesakes, because those publications do not appear to have been attended by all reasonable care.

36. Offer of amends. Where words have been published innocently as defined above, the publisher may make an offer of amends. As regards newspapers, this means (*s.* 4(3)) an offer "to publish, or join in the publication of, a suitable correction of the words complained of, and a sufficient apology to the party aggrieved in respect of those words".

The offer must be expressed to be made for the purpose of *s.* 4 of the Act, and must be accompanied by an affidavit showing that the publication was innocent. No other evidence will be admissible to prove innocent publication (*s.* 4(2)).

37. If offer is accepted. If the offer is accepted by the aggrieved party, and performed, "no proceedings for libel shall be taken or continued by that party against the person making the offer in respect of the publication in question (but without prejudice to any cause of action against any other person jointly responsible for that publication)".

Any steps to be taken in fulfilment of the offer will, in default of agreement, be decided by the High Court, which has power to award the aggrieved person his full costs and expenses.

38. If offer is refused. If the offer is not accepted, it is a defence, in any libel proceedings over the words complained of, to prove that they were published innocently in relation to the plaintiff, and that the offer was made as soon as practicable after the publisher had notice that they were, or might be, defamatory of the plaintiff, and had not been withdrawn.

This defence does not apply where the publisher is not the author of the words, unless he shows the author wrote them without malice.

"Publisher" includes any servant or agent of his who was concerned with the contents of the publication (*s.* 4(5)).

APOLOGY—LIBEL ACT 1843

39. Explanation. The *Libel Act* 1843, *s.* 2, enables the publisher of a newspaper or other periodical to plead that a libel was published without malice or gross negligence, and that, before commencement of the libel action, or at the earliest opportunity afterwards, he published a full apology or, if his publication appears at intervals exceeding one week, did so in any newspaper or periodical selected by the plaintiff.

A defendant may, on giving written notice of his intention to do so, give evidence, in mitigation of damages, of his offer to apologise. However, he cannot do so unless he has offered to the plaintiff a sum of money by way of amends (*Libel Act* 1845 *s.* 2).

40. Unpopular procedure. The procedure is seldom used, since a defendant would nowadays prefer to make a payment into court—so as to recover subsequent costs if a lesser sum is thereafter awarded as damages.

(The procedure should not be confused with the apology often given by a defendant in a statement in open court when a defamation action is settled.)

PROGRESS TEST 2

1. Enumerate the defences to a libel action. **(1)**

2. "Truth is a complete defence"—discuss. **(3)**

3. What requirements must be satisfied in order for the defence of absolute privilege to succeed in respect of a newspaper report of judicial proceedings? **(11–18)**

4. What is meant by "malice" in libel? **(24)**

5. "Comment must be based on facts known to the maker"—explain. **(30)**

6. Explain "matters of public interest". **(33)**

7. Explain the defence of unintentional defamation. **(34–38)**

CHAPTER III

LIBEL—REHABILITATION OF OFFENDERS ACT 1974

1. Explanation. This Act provides that certain offenders shall, after the lapse of a specified time, be deemed to be "rehabilitated", and be treated as if the offence had not been committed. Section 4(1):

". . . a person who has become a rehabilitated person for the purpose of this Act in respect of a conviction shall be treated for all purposes in law as a person who has not committed, or been charged with . . . the offence or offences which were the subject of that conviction . . ."

"(a) no evidence shall be admissible in any proceedings . . . to prove that any such person has committed or been charged with . . . any offence which was the subject of a spent conviction, and (b) a person shall not, in any such proceedings, be asked . . . any question relating to his past which cannot be answered without acknowledging or referring to a spent conviction . . . or any circumstances ancillary thereto."

NOTE: this section is subject to the provisions in **2** and **3**, below.

2. Effect on libel actions. Section 8 applies to any defamation action by a rehabilitated person "founded upon the publication of any matter imputing that the plaintiff has committed, or been charged with . . . an offence which was the subject of a spent conviction". A defendant may rely on any defence of justification, fair comment, or absolute or qualified privilege—except that he may not rely on a defence of justification unless publication was without malice (*s.* 8(5)), and he may not rely on the publication being a fair and accurate report of judicial proceedings "if it is proved that the publication contained a reference to evidence which was ruled to be inadmissible by virtue of *s.* 4(1)".

NOTE:
    (*i*) A single *reference* suffices to destroy the defence.

(*ii*) But the section refers to evidence which is *ruled* to be inadmissible, not merely wrongly admitted.

(*iii*) The restrictions apply only where the conviction had become spent before publication.

(*iv*) They do not apply to bona fide law reports not forming part of any other publication; or to publications for bona fide educational, scientific or professional purposes.

3. Admissible evidence. Evidence of "spent" convictions *may* be admitted (and if admitted, may be reported):

(*a*) in any criminal proceedings before a court in Great Britain (including any appeal or reference in a criminal matter);

(*b*) in service disciplinary proceedings, or appeals therefrom;

(*c*) in adoption, guardianship, etc., of minors, or the provision by any person of accommodation, care or schooling for them;

(*d*) where the rehabilitated person consents to the admission of such evidence;

(*e*) where the judicial authority is satisfied that justice cannot be done except by admitting or requiring evidence relating to a person's spent convictions.

Additionally, the *Rehabilitation of Offenders Act (Exceptions) Order* 1975 enables such questions to be asked in connection with a number of professions, including the law, medicine, dentistry, etc.

4. Definitions.

Judicial authority: ordinary courts of law, and any tribunal or body, including professional bodies, having power to determine any question affecting the rights, privileges, obligations or liabilities of any person, or to receive evidence affecting the determination of any such question.

Conviction: this includes a conviction by any court outside Great Britain, and any finding against a person (other than a finding linked with a finding of insanity) in any criminal proceedings, or in care proceedings under *s.* 1, *Children and Young Persons Act* 1969.

Sentence: any order made by a court in respect of a conviction, except (*a*) an order made in default of payment of a fine, or (*b*) an order dealing with a person in respect of a suspended sentence of imprisonment.

5. Rehabilitation—excluded sentences. Sentences excluded from rehabilitation are: life imprisonment; imprisonment or corrective training for more than 30 months; preventive detention; and detention during H.M. pleasure, or for life, or for more than 30 months, passed on certain young offenders convicted of murder, manslaughter, or wounding with intent to do grievous bodily harm.

6. Rehabilitation periods.

Sentence	Rehabilitation period
Imprisonment or corrective training for more than 6 and up to 30 months	10 years*
Cashiering, discharge with ignominy, or dismissal with disgrace, from the armed services	10 years*
Imprisonment for 6 months or less	7 years*
Dismissal from H.M. service	7 years*
Sentence of detention in respect of a conviction in service disciplinary proceedings	5 years*
Borstal training	7 years
Sentence of detention on young offender convicted under s. 53, Children and Young Persons Act 1933, or s. 57, C.Y.P. (Scotland) Act 1937 (murder, manslaughter, wounding with intent to do g.b.h.) for more than 6 but not more than 30 months	5 years
Order for detention in a detention centre	3 years
Absolute discharge	6 months
Conditional discharge, binding over to keep peace or be of good behaviour, or probation order	1 year (or, if longer, until expiry of the order)

Sentence	Rehabilitation period
Any of these orders on children or young persons: fit person order, care or supervision order; and, in Scotland: committal in custody to remand home, detention in place chosen by local authority, committal for residential training, approved school order, or a supervision requirement under the *Social Work (Scotland) Act* 1968	1 year (or, if longer, until expiry of the order)
Any of these orders in England or Wales: committal in custody to a remand home; approved school order; attendance centre order	Until 1 year after order expires
Order under *Mental Health Act* 1959 committing convicted person to mental hospital (with or without restriction of time)	5 years, or 2 years after expiry of order, whichever period is longer
Order imposing on a convicted person a disqualification, disability, etc.	Duration of the period of disqualification, etc.
Any fine or sentence not listed above	5 years*

(* These periods are subject to reduction by half for persons under 17.)

NOTE:
- (*i*) Consecutive terms of imprisonment are added together; concurrent or partly concurrent terms are not.
- (*ii*) The provisions apply also to suspended sentences. No account is taken of any variation of a suspended sentence which may be made by a court subsequently dealing with the offender; but where any sentence is reduced on appeal, the rehabilitation period is likely to be that applicable to the substituted sentence.
- (*iii*) A person does not become "rehabilitated" unless he has undergone his sentence; but he is not barred from rehabilitation through failure to pay a fine, or breach of a condition of a recognisance, or of a requirement in

relation to a sentence which renders him liable to be dealt with for the original offence; or of a suspended sentence or supervision order.

7. The Faulks Committee. The Faulks Committee in an interim report in 1974 said the Bill, as it then was, would, if passed in its then existing form, constitute "a serious and unjustifiable inroad into the freedom of the individual to tell the truth". Some subsequent modifications were made, but the Act still inhibits investigative journalism. (For other provisions of the Act, *see* X, **20** and XIX, **5**.)

PROGRESS TEST 3

1. What is a "rehabilitated person"? (**1**)

2. What defences are open to a newspaper in a libel action by a rehabilitated person arising from disclosure of a "spent" conviction? (**2**)

3. What sentences are excluded from rehabilitation? (**5**)

4. How does the Act apply to (*a*) suspended sentences, and (*b*) sentences which are reduced on appeal? (**6**)

5. What view did the Faulks Committee take of the Rehabilitation of Offenders Bill? (**7**)

CHAPTER IV

LIBEL—PROCEEDINGS

THE TRIAL

1. Jury trial. A party to a libel action has the right to claim jury trial unless the case involves voluminous documents (*Administration of Justice (Miscellaneous Provisions) Act* 1933, *s.* 6(1)). Even then, jury trial may be ordered where the public or parties' interests require it (*Rothermere* v. *Times Newspapers Ltd.* (1973)).

The Faulks Committee considered that jury trial should be ordered only where the court considered it to be in the interests of justice—and, even then, the judge should assess damages.

2. Functions of judge and jury. The judge decides whether the words are capable of bearing the alleged defamatory meaning (*Nevill* v. *Fine Art Co.* (1897)) and whether they are capable of enjoying privilege, or being a fair comment. The jury decides whether the words are defamatory of the plaintiff; whether the defences of privilege or fair comment are destroyed by malice; and the amount of any damages.

3. Criticisms of jury trial. The Faulks Committee found "much force" in criticisms that costs in jury actions were high, and juries' verdicts, and the damages they awarded, were "unpredictable".

In *McCarey* v. *Associated Newspapers Ltd.* (1965) where a doctor had been awarded £9,000, Lord Justice Diplock questioned why he should have that sum when a woman who lost a leg got only £2,000 from a jury.

In *Lewis* v. *Daily Telegraph Ltd.* (1961) libel damages of £100,000 were held on appeal to be "out of all proportion".

THE DAMAGES

4. Measure of damages. Damages for defamation should generally be compensatory, not punitive. Two House of Lords decisions (*Rookes* v. *Barnard* (1964) and *Cassell & Co. Ltd.* v. *Broome* (1972) have meant that punitive damages for defamation may now be awarded only where the defendant decided to publish and take the risk because the likely profit should exceed any libel damages.

A newspaper's good reputation can operate to its detriment in assessment of damages. In the *Lewis* case (*see* **3** above) Mr. Justice Salmon said the *Daily Telegraph* "enjoys a high reputation in the City, and the jury are entitled to take that into account".

Evidence of the plaintiff's *general* bad character (but not mere rumour) may be given to mitigate damages (*Plato Films Ltd.* v. *Speidel* (1961)).

Evidence may be given in mitigation of damages that the plaintiff has already recovered, or sought, damages for the publication of words to the same effect as those complained of —*Defamation Act* 1952, *s.* 12.

5. Contemptuous damages. Where the court is satisfied that the publication is defamatory, but no substantial damage has been done to the plaintiff in the circumstances, it will award contemptuous damages—usually the lowest coin in circulation. Examples: *Dering* v. *Uris* (1964) (doctor who carried out sterilisation operations in a concentration camp); *Brooks* v. *I.P.C. Newspapers Ltd.* (1974) (solicitor who spanked women's bottoms).

6. Who can be sued? Proceedings may be brought against the editor, contributor, printer or publisher, and vendor. A vendor has a good defence if he did not know the publication contained a libel (*Emmens* v. *Pottle* (1885)), but not if he ought to have known (*Vizetelly* v. *Mudie's Select Library* (1900)).

PROGRESS TEST 4

1. What are the respective functions of judge and jury in a libel action? **(2)**

2. "Libel damages should be compensatory, not punitive"— explain. **(4)**

3. What do you understand by "contemptuous damages"? **(5)**

4. Against which parties may an action for libel be brought? **(6)**

CHAPTER V

LIBEL AS A CRIME—MALICIOUS FALSEHOOD

LIBEL AS A CRIME

1. Criminal libel. This consists of the publication of words likely to so outrage reasonable persons as to cause a breach of the peace.

Truth is no defence, unless publication is for the public benefit (*Libel Act* 1843), and as words may wound more keenly if they are true than if they are untrue, the maxim is "the greater the truth, the greater the libel". Thus it is possible to publish a criminal libel of the dead, if it is such as to so wound the deceased's family as to provoke a breach of the peace.

Such proceedings are rare; if against a newspaper they require the leave of a High Court judge (*Law of Libel Amendment Act* 1888). In *R.* v. *Caunt* (1947) an editor wrote of Jews in Britain: "Violence may be the only way to bring them to their sense of responsibility." He said in court he meant thereby to warn the Jews of "what would eventually happen to them if they did not mend their ways". He was held not guilty of publishing a seditious libel (but see now *Race Relations Act* 1965 *s.* 6—see XVIII, **1**).

In 1977, a prosecution over an article in *Private Eye* was awaiting hearing (*R.* v. *Pressdram Ltd.* (1977)).

Blasphemous libels (vilifying or ridiculing God, and intended to outrage Christian feelings) and seditious libels (aimed at securing the overthrow of the established order by unlawful means, or inciting hostility between different classes of people) are criminal; but a scurrilous tirade, not merely a reasoned opinion, is required (*Bowman* v. *Secular Society* (1917)), and since such attacks are frequently made with (temporal) impunity, blasphemous and seditious libels may be said to be, in practice, dead letters.

MALICIOUS FALSEHOOD

2. Slander of goods. This consists of the *malicious* publication of a false statement disparaging the goods of another. The remedy is an action for damages, but special damage must be proved unless the words are *calculated* to cause the plaintiff pecuniary damage (*Defamation Act* 1952, *s.* 3). Mere *comparison* of another's goods with one's own does not suffice.

3. Slander of title. Here the mischief consists of a false statement disparaging another's title to his goods. The same rules apply as to slander of goods.

4. Malicious falsehood. Slander of goods and slander of title are two aspects of malicious falsehood, a tort whereby a person sustains pecuniary loss in consequence of a false statement maliciously published about him—e.g. that his business has closed down (*Ratcliffe* v. *Evans* (1892)).

PROGRESS TEST 5

1. Explain the maxim "the greater the truth, the greater the libel". **(1)**
2. What are the requirements of the tort of malicious falsehood? **(2, 3, 4)**

CHAPTER VI

CONTEMPT OF COURT

THE COURT AND THE JOURNALIST

1. Explanation. The law of contempt exists to deter or punish interference with the administration of justice or judicial proceedings, or acts tending to bring justice or the judiciary into disrepute.

Contempt in the face of the court consists of some unseemly conduct in the court room itself (e.g. shouting and singing— *Morris* v. *Crown Office* (1970)).

Journalistic contempts have been mostly the publication of material calculated to prejudice the conduct of legal proceedings which are pending or imminent, or to interfere with the administration of justice generally, or to scandalise the court.

2. Criminal and civil contempt.

(*a*) *Criminal contempt.* Criminal contempts are acts of a public character intended, or likely, to interfere with the administration of justice, e.g. by prejudicing a fair trial, intimidating witnesses, or bringing justice into disrepute.

(*b*) *Civil contempt.* Civil contempts consist of disobedience to court orders. They are of a private nature in that they affect only the parties to the litigation. Contempts by newspapers are almost invariably criminal contempts, though newspapers can commit civil contempt, if e.g., they incite or assist a person to do so. In *Attorney-General* v. *Dwyer and Rawle* (1975) a journalist was committed to prison for publicising a pop festival, the holding of which had been restrained by injunction.

(*c*) *Effective differences today.* Formerly no appeal lay in criminal contempts; this right is now provided by *s.* 13, *Administration of Justice Act* 1960. The Royal Prerogative to grant a free pardon still applies only to criminal contempts. Civil contempts may be punished by committal to prison for an indefinite period; where a person is imprisoned for a

31

criminal contempt, it must be (said Lord Parker in *Attorney-General* v. *Clough* (1963)) for a determinate period.

The remainder of this chapter is concerned with criminal contempts.

3. Meaning of "court". A court is any body with a duty to act judicially and a power to take evidence on oath. It includes a court martial (*R.* v. *Daily Mail, ex parte Farnsworth* (1921)), an ecclesiastical court (*R.* v. *Daily Herald, ex parte Bishop of Norwich* (1932)) and a tribunal of inquiry (*see* **29**).

4. Matters tending to prejudice a fair trial. A contempt is committed by the publication of matter prejudicial to a fair trial in pending or imminent proceedings.

The fact that a person has become so notorious that his past activities are known to almost everyone will not prevent a reference to his past from being prejudicial (*Jones* v. *D.P.P.* (1962)).

5. Intent to publish. There must be an intent to publish. Thus merely lending a newspaper containing contemptuous matter to another person, while unaware of its contents, has been held to be no contempt (*McLeod* v. *St. Aubyn* (1899)). (But *see* also *R.* v. *Griffiths*, **28**).

6. Irrelevance of intent to prejudice. Once an intent to publish is established, it is irrelevant, in the absence of reasonable care, that there was no intent to prejudice (but *see* **15** for a different view).

R. v. *Odhams Press Ltd.* (1957): *The People* published an article about the brothel-keeping activities of M, unaware that M had, the previous week, been arrested and charged with living off prostitutes. Lord Goddard said: "The test is whether the matter complained of is calculated to interfere with the course of justice, not whether such a result is intended."

NOTE: *s.* 11, *Administration of Justice Act* 1960, now provides that a publication shall not give rise to contempt if those responsible, having taken all reasonable care, did not know, and had no reason to suspect, that proceedings were pending or imminent.

7. There must be real risk of prejudice. In *Vine Products Ltd.* v. *Green* (1966) Mr. Justice Buckley said that not every discussion of some party's rights was automatically a contempt. "The risk that it will prejudice a fair trail must be a real and grave risk." Lord Parker said in *R.* v. *Duffy, ex parte Nash* (1960) that there must be a real risk, as opposed to a remote possibility.

Lord Reid in *Attorney-General* v. *Times Newspapers Ltd.* (1974) said the law of contempt exists "to prevent interference with the administration of justice, and should . . . be limited to what is reasonably necessary for that purpose".

8. Actual prejudice need not be proved. If there is a real risk of prejudice, it is no defence that no actual prejudice results. Lord Justice Cotton in *Hunt* v. *Clark* (1889) said: "It is not necessary that a judge or jury will be prejudiced, but if it is calculated to prejudice the proper cause, that is a contempt . . ."

Thus there may be contempt of criminal proceedings even if the accused is subsequently acquitted (*R.* v. *Evening Standard Co. Ltd.* (1954)).

9. Prejudice in favour of either party is contempt. Contempt may be equally committed by prejudicing criminal proceedings *in favour* of the accused, e.g. by campaigning for his acquittal (*R.* v. *Castro and others* (1873)). Campaigns in some left-wing newspapers for the acquittal of the "Shrewsbury Two" and others in 1973 would almost certainly, if proceedings had been taken, have been held to be contempts.

In 1976, the *Evening Standard* was fined £1,000 over a caption: "Hain—he's no bank robber" (*R.* v. *Evening Standard Co. Ltd.* (1976)).

10. Motivation for publication is irrelevant. In *R.* v. *Evening News* (1936), after the arrest of X on a charge of treason by possessing a firearm close to King Edward VIII, the *Evening News* said the incident had "no connection with any subversive movement". It was held that the words implied guilt of the accused, and constituted a contempt notwithstanding that the newspaper claimed to have published them to allay public anxiety.

11. Contempt in pictures. Contempt may consist of a photograph, especially if identity is a crucial issue.

The *Daily Mirror* carried a photograph of an accused on the morning when he was due to appear in an identity parade. HELD: the photograph could have prejudiced the identification if the potential witness had seen it before inspecting the parade. Lord Hewart said: "There is a duty to refrain from publication of a photograph *where it is apparent to a reasonable man that a question of identity arises*" (*R.* v. *Daily Mirror* (1927)).

In a Scottish case in 1960, when the *Daily Record* published a photograph of a well-known personality about to appear on an indecency charge, Lord Clyde adopted a different criterion:

"To pillory a well known individual charged with offences of this nature may be the sort of news that some types of newspaper think it good policy to purvey to the type of reader which that newspaper happens to attract, but to have done what this newspaper did constitutes a flagrant contempt of those principles of fair play which the Scottish press as a whole has always honourably observed."

This criterion was repeated in 1975 in Glasgow Sheriff Court, when newspapers published a pop star's photograph during his trial arising from a fatal road accident—although the Sheriff accepted that the pictures did not prejudice the trial.

In a murder trial, the judge directed that photographs of the accused, which had been used in evidence, should not be published until after the trial. A newspaper which published one of the photographs while the jury was deliberating was held not to be in contempt because publication was through a "bona fide mistake". The judge ruled that he had power to give such a *direction* where the photographs formed part of the evidence, but not otherwise (*R.* v. *Neilson* (1976)).

A contempt may equally consist of prejudice in a television programme (*R.* v. *Savundra* (1968); *Attorney-General* v. *London Weekend Television* (1973)).

12. When proceedings become "pending or imminent". "It is possible very effectually to poison the fountain of justice before it begins to flow"—Mr. Justice Wills in *R.* v. *Parke* (1903).

In *Stirling* v. *Associated Newspapers Ltd.* (1960), Lord Clyde said that once a crime had been *suspected*, the publication of *any* interview with *any* person in *any* way involved would "in all probability interfere with the course of justice and hinder a fair trial". Criminal investigations, he said, were for the police alone. In *R.* v. *Evening Standard, ex parte D.P.P.* (1924) an appeal to readers to act as detectives and investigate a crime had been held to be a contempt.

In *R.* v. *Beaverbrook Newspapers Ltd.* (1962) it was held that the words "pending *or* imminent" indicated that contempts could be committed of proceedings which were "imminent" as well as those which were "pending", so that disclosure of a suspect's antecedents at a time when a charge was likely would, unless excused by the remainder of *s.* 11, be a contempt.

In the *Savundra* case (*see* **11**) Savundra contended that his trial was prejudiced by a television interview with him. The court, though dismissing his appeal, made it clear that prejudicial matter published at a time when proceedings are imminent, though no charge has been brought, can be a contempt.

Proceedings are "pending" although there has been tardiness in bringing them to trial (*Attorney-General* v. *Times Newspapers Ltd.* (1974)).

A report by the Society of Conservative Lawyers in 1972 recommended reform of the law where proceedings were pending. No longer was anyone deceived by the euphemism "a man is helping police inquiries".

13. When proceedings cease to be "pending". Comment on the subject matter of a criminal proceeding, if published after conviction but before the hearing of an appeal, will constitute a contempt—said Lord Parker in *R.* v. *Duffy, ex parte Nash* (1960)—if there is a *clear intention* to prejudice the appeal. But he held that there was no contempt in publishing, after Nash's conviction but before the hearing of his appeal, matter highly disparaging of his character.

But Mr. Justice Humphreys warned in *R.* v. *Davies, ex parte Delbert Evans* (1945):

"While I would not suggest that it is likely that any judge as the result of information which had been improperly conveyed to him would give a decision which otherwise he would not have given, it is embarrassing to a judge that he should be informed of matters which he would much rather not hear, and which make it much more difficult for him to do his duty."

In *R.* v. *Gunn, ex parte Attorney-General* (1953) a contempt in the *Daily Sketch* consisted of a comment—after a finding by a court martial that a fusilier was guilty of cowardice—that "cowardice can no longer be treated as a simple crime". The finding was subject to confirmation, and Lord Goddard said the *object* of the article was to bring pressure on the confirming officer, and to influence his decision.

14. Prejudice in criminal cases. Since juries sit today mostly in criminal courts, it is from criminal proceedings that most newspaper contempt cases arise. Juries are much more likely than judges to be influenced by prejudicial material. Examples:

The *Daily Mirror* carried, on Haigh's arrest for murder, a story giving details of grisly killings which it said Haigh had committed. HELD: grave contempt, for which the editor was imprisoned (*R.* v. *Bolam, ex parte Haigh* (1949)).

A reporter covering an Assize trial telephoned to his newspaper evidence which had been given in committal proceedings. The Assize judge had ruled, in the jury's absence, that this evidence ought not to go before the jury. The reporter was not in court when the judge gave this ruling. HELD: contempt; and the fact that the accused was later acquitted was "neither here nor there" (*R.* v. *Evening Standard Co. Ltd.* (1954).)

NOTE:
  (*i*) Reporting of any proceedings heard in the absence of the jury is an obvious contempt. A "trial within a trial" is conducted in their absence to enable the judge to rule, e.g., on the admissibility of certain evidence, or whether two or more co-accused should have separate trials, without the jury's minds being prejudiced by those proceedings. To report those proceedings is to destroy the whole purpose of the exclusion of the jury.
  (*ii*) Previous convictions should not be reported on an application for bail (*R.* v. *Armstrong* (1951)).

15. Prejudice in civil cases. In *Re William Thomas Shipping Co. Ltd.* (1930) a judge said the view of a newspaper, "however intelligently conducted it might be", could not possibly affect a judge's mind. However, if there were an *intention* to prejudice the proceedings, there could be a contempt on that ground. Example:

The Sunday Times intended to publish an article on the drug Thalidomide at a time when claims for damages against the manufacturers, brought by children who had been damaged pre-natally by the drug, were still pending.

The newspaper had already published one article on the subject, and Lord Reid saw in it no offence against public policy, or pollution of the stream of justice, and the fact that it might have caused the manufacturers to do what they did not want to do (i.e. offer more compensation) was not, of itself, sufficient reason for saying it was a contempt.

The mere fact that litigation had begun need not inhibit discussion of general matters of public interest, such as the propriety of, e.g., local authorities evicting squatters from houses due for demolition; nor need it, he thought, inhibit discussion of a party's rights in a particular litigation—or even an attempt to urge a party to forgo his legal rights in whole or in part, though such urging would need to be done "in a fair and temperate way, and without any oblique motive".

But to prejudge a case, or specific issues in it, would be a contempt. He thought the proposed article would be a contempt. (*Attorney-General* v. *Times Newspapers Ltd.* (1974)).

Contrast *Attorney-General* v. *London Weekend Television Ltd.* (1973) where the High Court found no contempt in an L.W.T. programme about Thalidomide children because there was no *deliberate intention* to influence the pending proceedings and, in the circumstances, a single showing did not create a serious risk of interfering with the course of justice. But Lord Simon of Glaisdale, in the *Times Newspapers* case, thought there was here "at least a technical contempt".

16. Interlocutory proceedings. Interlocutory proceedings (i.e. where a party seeks relief pending the trial of a civil action) may be reported if heard in open court and, subject to **17**, below, if in chambers.

17. Hearings in private. Section 12, *Administration of Justice Act* 1960:

"(1) The publication of information relating to proceedings before any court sitting in private shall not of itself be a contempt of court except . . . (*a*) where the proceedings relate to wardship, adoption of any infant, or wholly or mainly to the guardianship, custody, maintenance or upbringing of an infant, or rights of access to an infant; (*b*) where the proceedings [concern a person

of unsound mind]; (c) where the court sits in private by reason
of national security during that part of the proceedings about
which the information is published; (d) where the information
relates to a secret process, discovery or invention which is in
issue in the proceedings; (e) where the court, having power to do
so, expressly prohibits the publication of all information relating
to the proceedings, or of information of the description which is
published.

"(2) . . . the publication of the text, or a summary of the
whole or part of an order made by a court sitting in private,
shall not of itself be a contempt of court except where the court,
having power to do so, expressly prohibits the publication".

NOTE:

    (i) A court sitting in private may be "in chambers" or "in
camera". When "in chambers", a court will hear matters
preliminary, or ancillary, to the action. Where the trial
of the action itself, or part of it, is heard in private, it
will be "in camera", not "in chambers".

    (ii) The words "the court having power to do so" suggest
there would be no contempt in disregarding a prohibition
which the court had no power to impose—but such an
argument did not find favour in the *Socialist Worker* case
(*see* **21**).

    (iii) In 1976 a judge held that *s.* 12 applied to disclosure of
any matter concerning a ward of court. On appeal, however, it was held there would be no contempt unless a
newspaper knew of the wardship, and the published
material related to it (*Re F, a minor* (1976)).

    (iv) In 1976, Mr. Justice Arnold warned that where children
were concerned, only the judge—not the parents—could
consent to publication.

18. Applications of s. 12. In *R.* v. *Prager* (1971), an official
secrets case, Lord Widgery, the Lord Chief Justice, warned that
it would be a potential contempt to speculate on what might
have gone on in court while it was sitting in camera. "It is just
as damaging if information of that kind can leak out as to have
the representatives of the press present and taking their notes
at the time."

During interlocutory proceedings in a case in 1959, a judge
said: "If I find that any reports are published purporting to say
what has happened before me in chambers I shall take steps to
see that the matter is reported to the appropriate authorities
for action. It is essential for the proper administration of justice

that statements should not be broadcast with regard to matters heard in chambers. Such matters concern the parties only, and no one else." (*Daily Telegraph*, 22nd December 1959).

That, however, was before the 1960 Act.

19. Payments into court. Frequently in civil actions the defendant pays a sum of money into court as an offer to dispose of the action. If the plaintiff refuses the offer, and the action goes forward to trial, the judge must not learn, before giving his judgment, the fact or amount of the payment. To publish this information before judgment is given is thus a contempt (*R.* v. *Wealdstone News Ltd.* (1925)).

20. Reports identifying protected persons. It would be a contempt of court to identify a ward of court (*see* X, **15**); or a patient under the *Mental Health Act* 1959 in proceedings before, e.g., the Court of Protection.

21. Reports prejudicial to the administration of justice generally. The *Socialist Worker* case: material tending to interfere with the administration of justice may constitute a contempt of court even if it does not prejudice the proceedings to which it relates.

Socialist Worker identified, during the trial of Janie Jones for blackmail (of which she was acquitted), the two alleged victims, in defiance of what was later held to be a *direction* by the judge that they be referred to only as "Mr. X" and "Mr. Y". The disclosure was held to be a contempt. Lord Widgery said that alleged victims in blackmail cases had for years been referred to anonymously. If they did not receive this protection they would be deterred from going to the police, since they would thereby receive the very publicity which they were prepared to pay to avoid (*R.* v. *Socialist Worker Printing and Publishing Co. Ltd.* (1974)).

22. Reports of judicial proceedings. A fair and accurate report of judicial proceedings (subject to restrictions in **17–21**) will not be a contempt notwithstanding that it may prejudice those, or other, proceedings. Examples:

The Recorder of London delivered a charge to a jury in a manner highly prejudicial to the accused. HELD: a newspaper was not in contempt by reporting the Recorder's ill-chosen words (*R.* v. *Evening News, ex parte Hobbs* (1925)).

Newspapers reported a trial at a time when the accused were awaiting trial on other charges. It was contended that the second trial was thereby prejudiced. But Mr. Justice Lawton said it would not be in the public interest if newspapers desisted from reporting trials merely because there was some other indictment still to be dealt with (*R.* v. *Kray* (1969)).

In a corruption trial, evidence was given referring to men awaiting trial in subsequent proceedings. Mr. Justice Waller said: "I do not see how the press can properly report this evidence without running the risk of being in contempt of this other trial" (*R.* v. *Poulson and Pottinger* (1974)). Mr. Justice Lawton's view (above) is likely to be preferred: it is more in line with the *Hobbs* decision (above).

23. Erroneous statements. In *R.* v. *Metropolitan Police Commissioner, ex parte Blackburn* (1968), a *Punch* article by Quintin Hogg, critical of the Court of Appeal, was said to be erroneous in one of its facts. "But errors do not make a contempt of court"—Lord Denning. Lord Justice Salmon said: "No criticism of a judgment, however vigorous, can amount to a contempt of court provided it keeps within the limits of reasonable courtesy and good faith."

24. Gagging writs. A gagging writ is one issued in order to inhibit comment on the facts forming its subject matter. In *Thomson* v. *Times Newspapers Ltd.* (1969) Lord Justice Salmon said it was a widely held fallacy that such a writ automatically stifled further comment. Such comment would not, in his view, amount to a contempt, though it might, if the editor had no defence, constitute a libel.

The Shawcross Committee had, in 1965, complained that the press was being harrassed by the lack of clarity of the law as to its freedom to comment on matters which were *sub judice*. The Committee had in mind the threats of contempt proceedings which had been made a year earlier by solicitors representing some of the accused in the Great Train Robbery.

In 1972 the Church of Scientology alleged contempt by the editor of *The Coventry Evening Telegraph* in publishing an editorial on Scientology at a time when libel actions by the Scientologists were pending. Mr. Justice O'Connor said the Scientologists were trying to stifle any criticism of their affairs. Their application was an abuse of the process of the court.

25. Scandalising the court. The right to comment on judicial decisions has been undoubted since *Ambard* v. *Attorney-General of Trinidad* (1936) where Lord Atkin said: "Justice is not a cloistered virtue. She must be allowed to suffer the scrutiny and respectful, even though outspoken, comments of ordinary men." This would not apply, he said, where improper motives were imputed to those administering justice.

In *R.* v. *Gray* (1900) a newspaper editor described a judge as "an impudent little man in horsehair", and "a microcosm of conceit and empty-headedness". The High Court, holding the article to be a contempt, said it went beyond criticism and was scurrilous, personal abuse of the judge himself.

In *Ambard's* case (above) criticism of apparent disparities between sentences passed in various courts was held not to be a contempt.

It is not so much the dignity of the judges themselves, as that of the court, which the law seeks to protect. Lord Widgery, in evidence before the Law Commission in 1971, said judges nowadays have to have "broad backs".

It is a contempt to question the impartiality of a judge:

> An article suggested that Dr. Marie Stopes, the birth control pioneer, "cannot apparently hope for a fair hearing in a court presided over by Mr. Justice Avory". HELD: a contempt. (*R.* v. *New Statesman Ltd., ex parte D.P.P.* (1928).)

But Borrie & Lowe, *The Law of Contempt*, suggest that "it is highly unlikely that allegations against judges in general, e.g. that they are biased against trade unions or in favour of their own class, amount to contempt".

THE SANCTIONS

26. Courts' punitive powers. A contempt in the face of the court (*see* 1) may be punished by the High Court or the Court of Appeal by imprisonment or fine; the sentence is at large (i.e. unlimited). A county court may impose a fine not exceeding twenty pounds or imprisonment not exceeding one month (*County Courts Act* 1959, *s.* 157). The Divisional Court of the Queen's Bench Division can, under its inherent supervisory jurisdiction, punish *all* cases of contempt of inferior courts. Its powers are at large.

The county court is powerless to deal itself with contempts

arising from prejudicial publications or scandalising of the court. In such cases (as in cases arising in magistrates' courts) an application for committal must be made to the Divisional Court.

27. Appeals. Since the *Administration of Justice Act* 1960, all persons held to be in contempt of court—civil or criminal— may now appeal. Appeals from the High Court (except the Divisional Court) and the county courts will go to the Court of Appeal. Appeals from the Divisional Court, and the Court of Appeal, will go to the House of Lords, if leave is obtained. Generally, leave will be granted only if a point of law of general public importance is involved.

28. Who may be dealt with? Writs of attachment for contempt of court may be issued against the writer or author, editor, printers, publishers, and even the distributors and vendors and the directors of the publishing company.

R. v. *Griffiths* (1957). An American magazine published material prejudicial to a murder trial in England. HELD: the U.K. distributors were in contempt, although they took all steps to stop circulation as soon as the matter was drawn to their attention. The newsvendors were also in contempt for selling the magazine, albeit innocently. (These parties now have the protection of *s.* 11, *Administration of Justice Act* 1960 (*see* **6**); the court indicted that proceedings were brought against them only because the real offender was abroad.)

R. v. *Bolam, ex parte Haigh* (1949) (*see* **14**). Lord Goddard said: "Let the directors beware. They now know the conduct of which their employees were capable, and the view which the court took of the matter. If for the purpose of increasing the circulation of their paper they should again venture to publish matter such as this, the directors themselves might find that the arm of the court is long enough to reach them and deal with them individually."

In *R.* v. *Evening Standard Co. Ltd.* (1954) (*see* **14**), Lord Goddard said it was a well understood rule of journalism that the editor and proprietors took responsibility in such cases, and he declined to accept a suggestion that they should not be held vicariously liable for the mistake or misconduct of their reporter.

In *R.* v. *Odhams Press Ltd.* (1957) (*see* **6**), the court "regretted" the attitude of the editor of *The People*, "who seemed to think it was no concern of his, and that he was entitled to rely on his reporter without more".

ABERFAN—AND AFTER

29. Contempt of inquiry tribunals: the Salmon Committee. An inter-departmental committee considered in 1969 the contempt powers of tribunals of inquiry, including the case of *Attorney-General* v. *Mulholland and Foster* (1963) (*see* **XI, 2**) where journalists were imprisoned for refusing to identify their sources before the Vassall Tribunal.

The 1969 Committee sat soon after the controversy over the tribunal set up to investigate the Aberfan coal-tip disaster, when the Attorney-General and Lord Chancellor of the day both warned that any trespass by the media on matters which the tribunal had to investigate would be a contempt. The Committee considered that tribunals of inquiry (these are tribunals set up in compliance with a resolution of both Houses of Parliament—not administrative tribunals, such as those dealing with pensions, Social Security, etc.) enjoyed powers not enjoyed by other types of tribunal; that an interview with a prospective witness before a tribunal of inquiry would be a contempt; and that the mere conducting of the interview itself might be a contempt if the witness were bullied in such a way as might deter him from giving evidence.

A tribunal of inquiry may thus take steps in cases of contempt such as may the High Court, except that it has no power of its own to commit the offender to prison. It can merely certify to the High Court its view that the person concerned is in contempt (*s.* 2(1), *Tribunals of Inquiry (Evidence) Act* 1921). The High Court may then agree or disagree. It does not, said Lord Parker in *Attorney-General* v. *Clough* (1963) merely rubber-stamp the tribunal's view.

FUTURE OUTLOOK

30. Proposed changes: the Phillimore Report. Wide-ranging proposals to clarify and liberalise the law of contempt were made by the Phillimore Committee, which reported in 1974.

The Committee recommended clarification of the law so as to allow as much freedom as possible consistent with maintaining the citizen's rights to a fair and unimpeded system of justice, and protecting the orderly administration of the law. The report recommended the abolition of all distinctions between civil and criminal contempt. It pointed to the uncertainty as to whether publications were at risk when proceedings were "imminent"; it recommended that a publication should give rise to strict liability in the law of contempt only if it created a risk that the courts would be seriously impeded or prejudiced, and that, in criminal proceedings in England and Wales, strict liability should apply only where the accused person was charged or a summons served and, in civil proceedings, only if the case had been set down for trial.

Liability should cease when verdict and sentence are pronounced, or judgment given, or an equivalent order or decree made or given. If a jury failed to agree, the restriction should continue to apply until the re-trial was over, or until it was clear that it would not take place.

Within those limits, publication of any matter creating a risk of justice being seriously impeded or obstructed should be contempt without proof of intent to impede or obstruct.

The defence of innocent publication in *s*. 11, *Administration of Justice Act* 1960, should continue; and it should be a defence to show that the material complained of was a fair and accurate report of legal proceedings in open court published contemporaneously and in good faith.

Scandalising the court should cease to be a part of the law of contempt; it should be an indictable offence to defame a judge in such a way as to bring the administration of justice into disrepute. It should be a defence to prove that the allegations were true and publication was for the public benefit.

NOTE: The Law Commission, in its Working Paper 62, made a broadly similar recommendation, but said it was "much alive to the juridical difficulties of such a defence".

The Phillimore Committee also called for an inquiry into the practice of offering witnesses in criminal trials money for their stories, subject to the accused being convicted—something which came to light in evidence in the "Moors" murder trial (*R*. v. *Brady and Hindley* (1966)).

Dealing with the *Socialist Worker* case (*see* 21) the Committee called for legislation to provide that in specific circumstances such as this the court should be empowered to prohibit, in the public interest, the publication of names *or other matters* arising at a trial.

PROGRESS TEST 6

1. For what purpose does the law of contempt exist? **(1)**

2. Distinguish between civil and criminal contempt. **(2–4, 30)**

3. Explain the defence under *s*. 11, *Administration of Justice Act* 1960. **(6)**

4. Explain the requirements of prejudice in contempt of court. **(6–9)**

5. In what circumstances is publication of a photograph likely to give rise to a contempt of court? **(11)**

6. Explain the meaning of "pending or imminent" proceedings. **(11, 12)**

7. What was the effect of the decision in *Attorney-General* v. *Times Newspapers Ltd*. (1974)? **(12, 15)**

8. What benefits do journalists derive from *s*. 12, *Administration of Justice Act* 1960? **(17)**

9. What was the effect of the decision in the *Socialist Worker* case, 1974? **(21)**

10. What is a "gagging writ"? What, according to Lord Justice Salmon, is its effect? **(24)**

11. Is a newspaper likely to be in contempt by commenting: "Judges do not know how working people live"? **(25)**

12. Does a person who is held to be in contempt have a right of appeal? **(27)**

13. Is a newspaper editor the only person who may be dealt with for contempt of court? **(28)**

14. Does a tribunal of inquiry have powers to commit a person to prison for contempt of court? **(29)**

15. Mention some of the principal changes recommended by the Phillimore Committee. **(30).**

CHAPTER VII

BREACH OF PRIVILEGE—OR CONTEMPT—OF PARLIAMENT

1. Explanation. Breach of privilege and contempt may be taken for *practical* purposes to be synonymous (though the penal jurisdiction of Parliament extends to all contempts, whether or not they violate any specific privileges of either House). The Select Committee on Parliamentary Privilege recommended in 1968 that "contempt of Parliament" should be substituted for "breach of privilege", to remove any suspicion that M.P.s wished to be a privileged class.

Contempt of Parliament is in many ways analogous to contempt of court, but the alleged offender has no right of being heard, of legal representation, or of appeal.

Contempt of Parliament may consist of, e.g., unseemly conduct in the precincts of either House while the House is sitting; words reflecting on either House; acts or words tending to obstruct, intimidate, or improperly influence Members of either House in the discharge of their duties; wrongful disclosure of confidential information; or misrepresenting proceedings.

2. Unseemly conduct. In 1947, after an altercation between a Press Gallery journalist and an M.P., both men were held by the Committee of Privileges to be in contempt.

3. Words reflecting on either House. ". . . indignities offered . . . by words spoken or writings published reflecting on its character or proceedings have been constantly punished by both the Lords and the Commons upon the principle that such acts tend to obstruct the Houses in the performance of their functions by diminishing the respect due to them." (Erskine May, *Parliamentary Practice*, 19th Edn.)

Examples of this kind of contempt:

1957, *Sunday Express* and *Romford Recorder*: their respective editors were called to the Bar of the Commons after their newspapers had alleged—on the Committee's finding—that M.P.s had favoured themselves in petrol allocations during the fuel shortage consequent on the Suez invasion. Both were held to be in breach of privilege. The *Romford Recorder* editor protested in vain to the Press Council that his treatment had been unfair, and that he had published the truth; but truth is no defence.

1953, Mrs. Patricia Ford M.P., in the *Sunday Express*: she wrote that she had seen two women M.P.s "asleep and snoring" in a rest room at the House. HELD: breach of privilege.

1975, *Travel Trade Gazette*: an article questioned the motives of an M.P. in speaking on the second reading of the **Air** Transport Reserve Fund Bill. HELD: a serious contempt, "not only reflecting on the House but tending to undermine freedom of speech in Parliament".

1947, *World's Press News*: Garry Allighan M.P. wrote that M.P.s had been conveying confidential information to newspapers for payment. An inquiry by the Committee of Privileges revealed transactions between two M.P.s—one of them Allighan himself —and two newspapers. Allighan was expelled from the House. The second Member—and the *W.P.N.* editor—were admonished.

1887, *The Times*: surprisingly, the Speaker did not hold a *prima facie* breach of privilege in a statement that certain Members "draw at once their living and their notoriety from the steady perpetration of crimes for which civilisation demands the gallows".

It may even be a contempt to comment adversely on a decision of the Committee of Privileges.

"The situation is obscure, but the risk is worth taking. The recent reports from the Committee underline the need to ventilate the general question of the relation between Parliamentary privilege and the right of the Press and individuals freely to criticise the actions of their representatives in Parliament."— *The Times*, 27th March 1957.

4. Acts tending to obstruct, etc., Members. "The real test is that nothing ought to be done which is calculated to put a Member in such fear of consequences if he speaks or acts in a particular way that he will refrain from speaking or acting in that way"—Sir Hartley Shawcross, Attorney-General, 1947.

Examples:

1967, *Town* magazine: an article on the Free Wales Army reported threats to the lives of two Members for "selling out" Wales. HELD: contempt.

1957, *Sunday Graphic*: This newspaper, incensed by a Parliamentary question by Arthur Lewis M.P., stated: "If you agree with us . . . ring up Mr. Lewis and tell him." It gave Mr. Lewis's telephone number, and he was for days pestered by calls. HELD: contempt.

Sponsored M.P.s: the Committee has appeared to recognise that many Members look after the interests of outside bodies (e.g. trade unions) but there are limits to the pressure to which they may be subjected. In 1974, only the tactful intervention of Kenneth Morgan, General Secretary of the National Union of Journalists, smoothed over a complaint about a member of that Union who had sought to institute disciplinary proceedings against a union member M.P. for the way he had voted in Parliament.

5. Wrongful disclosure, etc., of information. Although, after the Allighan case (*see* **3**) the House expressed its "grave displeasure" at the offering of payment to a Member for the disclosure of confidential information, such action was not held to be a breach of privilege or contempt.

But in 1968 a Member was reprimanded for giving to *The Observer* evidence given to a Select Committee at Porton Down.

In 1972, the *Daily Mail* was held to be in contempt in publishing information about proposed increased payments to the Royal Family, the information being in many respects identical to that in a confidential draft report. Gordon Greig, the *Daily Mail* political correspondent, apologised. The Committee said the principal offender was the supplier of the information who—Mr. Greig having refused to name him—remained undetected. (A motion to suspend Mr. Greig from lobby facilities for a month was lost on the chairman's casting vote.)

In 1975 the Committee recommended excluding *The Economist* editor and a contributor from lobby facilities for six months for publishing details from a Select Committee's draft report on the wealth tax. The recommendation was not implemented.

When a Select Committee was set up in 1976 to investigate certain allegations about M.P.s, the Attorney-General warned that identifying persons entering or leaving the room where the Committee was sitting would be a contempt.

6. Misrepresenting proceedings. In 1701 the Commons resolved that misrepresenting proceedings in Parliament was a breach of privilege, and committed the offender to the Tower.

It is thought that the misrepresentation would need to be wilful in order to offend against this resolution. In 1971 the House of Commons rescinded a resolution of 1762 whereby *all* unauthorised reports of its proceedings were technically a breach of privilege; but it is still a breach if the proceedings are in private, or expressly prohibited to the press.

7. Discourtesy no breach of privilege. In 1972 a newspaper purported to give a Committee's findings on the wish of the Defence Under-Secretary (Air Force) to continue to be called "Lord Lambton" in the Commons. The Speaker said it was a "discourtesy" to the House, but felt unable to rule that there was a *prima facie* breach of privilege.

In Mrs. Ford's case (*see* 3) the Committee of Privileges said it was not its function to decide on the *taste* of an article.

8. Procedure in case of breach of privilege or contempt. Where a complaint is founded on something published in a newspaper or book, the complaining Member delivers a copy at the table. The Speaker will rule, perhaps reserving his decision, whether a *prima facie* breach of privilege is made out such as to justify priority over the Orders of the Day. If so, the matter goes to the Committee of Privileges. Generally, where the Committee recommends that no breach of privilege has occurred, no proceedings are taken.

If there is a breach, the offender may be admonished or reprimanded, or detained in custody until not later than the prorogation of that Parliament. He may also be fined—a sanction not exercised since 1666. If a Member, he may be expelled by a resolution of Members, as was Allighan (*see* 3).

9. Committee's guidance. In 1975 the Committee advised Members that the House's penal jurisdiction should be invoked only where essential to provide reasonable protection for the House, its Members or officers, and never in respect of trivial complaints, or where the complainant has a remedy in the courts, particularly if the complaint concerns an alleged defamatory statement.

10. Reform of the law governing Parliamentary contempts. In 1968 the Select Committee on Parliamentary Privilege recommended that "contempt of Parliament" be substituted for "breach of privilege"; that where an M.P. has a remedy in the courts he should not be permitted to invoke the penal jurisdiction of the House (*cf.* the guidance in **9**, above); that a person or newspaper accused of contempt be allowed legal respresentation before the investigating committee, with legal aid where appropriate; and that, although the present inquisitorial procedure had its defects, the House should retain the power to judge and punish serious attacks on the House of Commons or individual Members which obstruct them in carrying out their Parliamentary functions.

Professor Harry Street (*Freedom, the Individual and the Law*) disagrees with the last recommendation. He writes: "Let the ordinary courts decide when the freedom of the press should be curtailed in the interests of the legislature, and let the accused have his trial by jury in those courts of law."

PROGRESS TEST 7

1. Give examples of the forms which contempt of Parliament may take. **(1)**

2. On what principles do the Houses of Parliament punish "indignities" which are published about them? **(3)**

3. Are all unauthorised reports of proceedings in the Commons a breach of privilege? **(3)**

4. What is the "real test" for complaints arising from intimidation, etc., of Members? **(4)**

5. Is a newspaper editor at risk in publishing confidential information from a draft report circulated to Ministers? **(5)**

6. If so, what sanctions may the House levy against him? **(8)**

7. Outline the recommendations of the Select Committee on Parliamentary Privilege. **(10)**

CHAPTER VIII

ADMISSION TO MEETINGS OF PUBLIC BODIES

1. Explanation. Since 1908 pressmen have been entitled to attend local authority meetings. Admission rights have since been extended to local authority committee meetings, and meetings of certain other public bodies. But there are qualifications, and the statutory provisions can still be circumvented.

2. Development. In 1908 a newspaper editor who had been excluded from meetings of his local council claimed to be entitled to admission, both as a journalist and as a ratepayer. The High Court held he was not entitled to admission in either capacity (*Tenby Corporation* v. *Mason* (1908)).

The decision moved Parliament to pass the *Local Authorities (Admission of Press to Meetings) Act* 1908, giving the press, but not the public, a right to attend local authority meetings, subject to the council's power to go into committee to discuss confidential business. That Act was repealed by the *Public Bodies (Admission to Meetings) Act* 1960, which gave both press and public a right to attend meetings of local authorites and other specified public bodies. The *Local Government Act* 1972 extended the admission rights to local authority committees.

3. Bodies to whose meetings the public must be admitted. Under the 1960 Act, as amended by the *Local Government Act* 1972, the *National Health Service Reorganisation Act* 1973, the *Water Act* 1973 and the *Community Land Act* 1975, these are: county councils, district councils, city councils, borough councils, the Greater London Council, and London boroughs; the Land Authority for Wales; parish councils and parish meetings; community councils and community meetings (in Wales); regional health authorities, area health authorities and community health councils; water authorities; education committees, including joint education committees and divisional executives; and any bodies, other than police authorities, with the power to levy a rate.

The Secretary of State may, by statutory instrument, add other bodies to this list (*s.* 2(3)).

A meeting of a committee of a public body will, if the committee includes all the members of that body, be treated for these purposes as if it were a meeting of the body itself. The provision is now somewhat academic so far as local authorities are concerned, in view of the right of admission to committees.

In 1958 a District Auditor refused to hear an objection to a council's accounts in public. Section 159, *Local Government Act* 1972, which provides the right of objection, does not stipulate that the hearing must be in public.

4. Shutting out the press. The 1960 Act, *s.* 1(1), makes the rights of admission conferred by that Act subject to *s.* 1(2), which enables a public body, by resolution, to exclude the public from a meeting, whether during the whole or part of the proceedings, "whenever publicity would be prejudicial to the public interest by reason of the confidential nature of the business to be transacted, or for any other special reasons stated in the resolution and arising from the nature of that business or of the proceedings".

Where such a resolution is passed, the public and press may be excluded "during the proceedings to which the resolution applies".

Note that there may be no exclusion until an appropriate resolution has been passed. In 1968 Linda Preece, a trainee reporter, refused to leave a parish council meeting until such a resolution was passed. When the motion was proposed and voted on, it was rejected; and Linda stayed. The chairman said one local paper had published an inaccurate previous story on the matter about to be discussed. This reason, whether true or not, would not have been a valid ground for going into committee.

In 1971 reporters were excluded from a meeting of West Mersea U.D.C. The Press Council "regretted" that the resolution did not state why publicity would be prejudicial to the public interest. (The Act, strictly construed, requires the reason to be stated only if the reason falls within the words "other special reasons".)

The courts will not set aside a resolution by reason only of the non-statement of the reason, unless a person's interests have been injured (*R.* v. *Liverpool Corporation* (1974)).

During the 1959 strike by printers employed on Newspaper Society papers, some councils refused to admit reporters because they felt reporters should not assist to produce newspapers during the strike. M.P.s were told that the government's interpretation of the 1908 Act—which in this respect was similar to the 1960 Act—was that when the press were excluded for reasons other than the special nature of the business "a council is open to challenge in the courts", and "an injunction could be sought to restrain a council from excluding representatives of the press except in the circumstances prescribed in the Act".

In 1975 the Ombudsman adjudicated that exclusion of press and public from a meeting of a district council while the council considered a planning application from a local dignitary "could well give rise to suspicion and rumour", though he acquitted the council of maladministration. He said suspicion was unlikely to be allayed by the absence of a written report to the appropriate committee. The only indication of how the matter was discussed was in the brief formal minute of the decision.

In 1967 Bournemouth Council went into committee to discuss a report by management consultants. The Press Council thought this step appeared "improper". The 1960 Act provides that the need to receive or consider recommendations or advice from sources other than the public body's own members, committees or sub-committees, may be treated as a "special reason" for going into committee; but makes it clear that this does not mean that reports from the council's own members, committees, etc., cannot be "special reasons".

5. Newspaper's right to receive minutes. A public body is required on request, and on payment of postage or other necessary charge for transmission, to supply for the benefit of any newspaper a copy of the agenda for the meeting. The copy supplied must be "as supplied to the members of the body—but excluding, if thought fit, any item during which the meeting is likely not to be open to the public".

Local authorities have from time to time sought to elicit from local newspapers undertakings that no information appearing in the minutes or reports of committees shall be published until it is considered by the full council. An official circular sent to local authorities in 1975 stated: "There should be no embargo to prevent reports and comments being made in advance of the meeting."

The section does not say expressly that the agenda must reach the newspaper several days before the meeting—though by implication it must mean that it should arrive before the meeting. An official circular issued to local authorities in May 1961 said: "Where the press are admitted to a meeting, they should be able to obtain *advance* information about the business to be discussed."

The 1975 circular mentioned above stated that the press should have copies of documents circulated to council and committee members, and "these should usually reach the press at the same time as they reach members, but if this cannot be done, the press should still get them in sufficient time to form a clear understanding of the matters under discussion".

NOTE: These circulars contain mere recommendations, not directions. While some councils comply by convention, others do not.

The section further requires that newspapers be supplied with "such further statements or particulars, if any, as are necessary to indicate the nature of the items included, or, if thought fit in the case of any item, with copies of any reports or other documents supplied to members of the body in connection with the item".

Section 160(2), *Local Government Act* 1972, provides that the agenda supplied to the members of a public body, for a meeting of that body at which an auditor's report is to be considered, shall be accompanied by the report, "and the report shall not be excluded from the matter supplied for the benefit of any newspaper" under the 1960 Act.

NOTE: *Any* elector may inspect a local authority's minutes and abstract of accounts, and make copies from them (*s.* 228, *Local Government Act* 1972). *Any* "person interested" may inspect the accounts at audit (*s.* 159).

6. Press accommodation and facilities. Section 1(4) of the *Public Bodies (Admission to Meetings) Act* 1960 states:

"While the meeting is open to the public, the body shall not have power to exclude members of the press from the meeting, and duly accredited representatives of newspapers attending for the purpose of reporting the proceedings for their newspapers shall, so far as practicable, be afforded reasonable facilities for taking their report and, unless the meeting is held in premises not belonging to the body or not on the telephone, for telephoning their report at their own expense."

7. Facilities extend to all "media". The rights and facilities set out in **3–6** above apply also to news agencies, and to any organisations which are systematically engaged in collecting news for sound or television broadcasts (*s.* 1(7)).

8. Photography, etc., excluded. The Act does not require the permitting of the taking of photographs, the use of sound or visual recording or transmission equipment, or the making of an oral commentary on the proceedings.

9. Disorderly behaviour. The right of the public to attend and remain at the meeting shall "be without prejudice to any power of exclusion to suppress or prevent disorderly conduct or other misbehaviour at a meeting" (*s.* 1(8)). At least one local authority construes this provision as enabling it, in the event of a disturbance, to invoke its standing orders which purport to give it a power to sit in private.

10. Admission to committees. Before 1973, only one local authority in ten opened all its committees to the press (Report by the Institute of Public Relations, 1972). Only their education committees were obliged to meet in public. As a result, ratepayers frequently did not hear of important proposals until it was too late to object.

Section 100, *Local Government Act* 1972, now provides: "For the purpose of securing the admission so far as practicable of the public (including the press) to all meetings of committees of local authorities, as well as to the meetings of the local authorities themselves, the [1960 Act] shall have effect subject to the following provisions of this section."

The "following provisions" referred to are that the admission rights shall apply also to any joint committees established by two or more local authorities, and to such bodies as police committees, children's committees, regional planning committees, and committees dealing with social services, local government superannuation, and national parks.

At meetings of such committees, the press must, "so far as practicable", be provided with the facilities mentioned in **6** above.

11. Admission to sub-committees. The 1975 circular mentioned in **5** above also states: "The law says nothing either way about the admission of the public and press to meetings of sub-committees . . . . meetings of sub-committees should be treated in the same way as other meetings, particularly where they have delegated powers. If decisions affecting the public are taken, the public ought to know what is decided, and why . . . . If it is decided, on cogent grounds, that a sub-committee should not transact its business in public, it becomes the more important that, to the maximum extent permitted by the nature of the matter involved, its reports to the parent committee or council should be fully explanatory, and should be available to the public and press."

12. Meetings of non-public bodies. Bodies which are not required by statute to conduct their business in public (e.g. trades councils, ratepayers' associations) are not obliged to admit the press, and may require reporters to leave at any time. If requested to leave, a reporter's licence to attend is thereby revoked, and if he refuses he may be removed with no greater force than necessary. The only possible answer—barely tenable —might be that in some circumstances the reporter is not a "bare licensee", but has a licence coupled with an interest.

PROGRESS TEST 8

1. List some of the public bodies to which the *Public Bodies* (*Admission to Meetings*) *Act* 1960 gives a right of admission. **(3)**

2. Must objections to local authorities' expenditure be heard in public? **(3)**

3. In what circumstances may a local authority resolve to go into committee? **(4)**

4. Is alleged inaccurate reporting a ground for excluding the press from a council meeting? **(4)**

5. How can the press enforce, if necessary, its right to attend council meetings? **(4)**

6. Are journalists entitled to receive council minutes? **(5)**

7. Are they entitled to receive any other council documents? **(5)**

8. Are they entitled to seats in the well of the council chamber? **(6)**

9. Are they entitled to take photographs at council meetings? **(8)**

10. Explain journalists' rights of admission, if any, to (*a*) committees and (*b*) sub-committees, of local authorities. **(10, 11)**

CHAPTER IX

ADMISSION TO COURTS

ADMISSION RIGHTS—GENERALLY

1. Explanation. "I am of opinion that every court of justice is open to every subject of the King"—Lord Halsbury in *Scott* v. *Scott* (1913).

"Unless there are compelling reasons to the contrary, any judicial proceedings should be conducted in the full glare of publicity"—Lord Parker, Lord Chief Justice, speaking on the Criminal Justice Bill 1967.

In *R.* v. *Sussex Justices, ex parte McCarthy* (1924) Lord Hewart, albeit in a different context, used words which have attained immortality: ". . . justice should not only be done, but should manifestly and undoubtedly be seen to be done".

Many proceedings, however, may be conducted in private. To others, the press, but not the public, are admitted. (*See* also Chapter X for restrictions on reporting.)

2. Reasons for sitting in private. Courts may sit in private in the interests of national security; to protect patents and trade secrets; in various cases involving, e.g., adoption, guardianship of minors, legitimacy, wardship; in proceedings by a petitioning spouse for an injunction pending the hearing of a petition before a divorce court; during evidence of sexual capacity in medical nullity suits; and where the court is satisfied that justice cannot otherwise be done.

3. Invalid reasons. In *Scott* v. *Scott* (1913), Viscount Haldane said: "A mere desire to consider feelings of delicacy, or to exclude from publicity details which it would be desirable not to publish, is not enough. . . . I think that to justify an order for a hearing in camera, it must be shown that the paramount object of securing that justice is done would really be rendered doubtful of attainment if the order were not made."

The fact that publicity may deter a litigant is not a sufficient reason for sitting *in camera* (*Greenway* v. *Attorney-General* (1927)); nor are a parent's fears that publicity may harm his child's well-being (*B.* v. *Attorney-General* (1965)).

Indecency of evidence is not generally a ground for excluding the press (*see* **4** and **17** below). In *E.* v. *E.* (1963) a court would not hear, *in camera*, a wife's evidence of alleged sodomy.

4. No power to exclude from indecency cases. Section 37, *Children and Young Persons Act* 1933, provides that, in proceedings for an offence involving conduct contrary to decency or morality in which a witness is called who, in the opinion of the court, is a child or young person, the court may direct that persons other than those concerned in the conduct of the case be cleared from the court. But the section adds the proviso:

"Provided that nothing in this section shall authorise the exclusion of *bona fide* representatives of a newspaper or news agency."

The Windsor Express case: in 1952, a juvenile court refused to admit Elizabeth Bailey, a reporter of the *Windsor, Slough & Eton Express*, to a hearing where five boys were accused of sexual offences against a girl of twelve. When the case was resumed three weeks later, reporters demanded admission—on legal advice—and the newspaper was represented by Lord Hailsham, who put two submissions to the magistrates:

(*i*) that any decision reached with the press wrongfully excluded would not be the decision of "the juvenile court", and would be voidable;

(*ii*) that any police officer who obeyed illegal instructions to forcibly remove a representative of the press might find himself liable for damages for assault (*cf.* Mr. Garlick in **17** below).

The Bench agreed that the press should remain. Some of the reasons advanced for excluding the press were singularly lacking in any cogency: e.g. that the girl was under 13; that "it wouldn't do any good if printed in the paper"; that their exclusion powers were "as wide as possible". Lord Hailsham pointed out the proviso to *s.* 37 (exempting journalists) and the House of Lords decision in *Scott* v. *Scott* (*see* **1**).

5. Disorderly conduct. In *Scott* v. *Scott* (1913) Lord Loreburn said disorder, or just apprehension of it, in a court would justify the exclusion or partial exclusion of the public. The remainder of his speech suggests, though the point is not clear, that such exclusion should extend only to those causing the disorder.

THE SUPERIOR COURTS

6. House of Lords. The law lords, having laid down the public's rights of admission to courts (*Scott* v. *Scott* (1913): *see* **1** and **3** above) observe those rights in their own court.

7. The High Court and Court of Appeal. These, with the Crown Court, form the Supreme Court of Judicature (*Courts Act* 1971, *s.* 1). The High Court consists of the three Divisions in **11, 12** and **13** below.

8. Admission. The *Supreme Court of Judicature (Consolidation) Act* 1925, *s.* 61(2), states: "A judge of the High Court sitting in court shall be deemed to constitute a court of the High Court." "In court", it is submitted, means "in open court".

In *Stone* v. *Stone* (1949) Lord Justice Bucknill said:

> "I am satisfied that a decree made in a judge's private room is not a valid decree. It is voidable because it offends against the fundamental rule that the hearing of a case, and the whole case, must take place in open court.
>
> "The only ground on which an exception is made to that rule is where justice cannot be done unless the case is heard in private."

Thus the general rule is that the High Court—and the Court of Appeal (*Re Agricultural Industries Ltd.* (1952))—must sit in open court except where they have express power by statute (e.g. **2** above), by statutory instrument or the Rules of the Supreme Court, or at common law, to sit in private.

9. Committal from a hearing in private. In 1967 Raymond Hughes, a High Court reporter, noticed that a man was being removed to prison after committal there at a hearing *in camera* for contempt of court in relation to a girl ward of court. Press protests produced an amendment of Order 52, rule 6, *Rules of the Supreme Court*. The rule now preserves the court's power to hear such proceedings *in camera* (together with cases under the *Mental Health Act* 1959, and cases where national security or the administration of justice might otherwise be injuriously affected) but adds:

> "If the court hearing an application in private . . . decides to make an order of committal against the person sought to be committed, it shall in open court state: (*a*) the name of the person; (*b*) in general terms the nature of the contempt . . . and (*c*) if he is being committed for a fixed period, the length of that period."

10. Appellate proceedings. *Domestic and Appellate Proceedings (Restriction of Publicity) Act* 1968 provides that where an appeal, or an application for leave to appeal, is brought against a decision of a court which had the power to sit in private, the appeal, or any part of it, may also be heard in private (*s.* 1(1)).

But if the appellate court does sit in private, it must give its decision in public, unless there are "good and sufficient" reasons for giving them in private; in that case the court must state in public what the "good and sufficient" reasons are (*s.* 1(2)).

The Act applies to appeals from the Court of Appeal, the High Court, the Restrictive Practices Court, county courts and magistrates courts.

Note that the appellate court has the power, not an obligation, to sit in private. In practice the Court of Appeal tends to admit the press to appeals in, e.g., wardship and cases involving minors, under a long-standing gentlemen's agreement that the minors will not be identified.

Where an application is made for an appellate court to sit in private, the application itself shall be heard in private unless the court otherwise directs (*s.* 1(5)).

This power to sit in private is in addition to any other such power it may have (*s.* 1(6)).

11. Chancery Division. Proceedings in chambers are in private, though a judge may give a decision in open court if it involves a point of law or procedure which he wishes reported (generally for lawyers' benefit rather than that of the press). Motions for interlocutory injunctions (temporary injunctions pending the hearing of an action), however, are heard in open court (contrast interlocutory proceedings in the Queen's Bench Division, **12** below); often the trial of a motion is treated, by consent of the parties, as the trial of the action.

All other proceedings are in open court, except evidence and submissions in cases involving secret products, processes, etc., in the Patent Court (*Badische Anilin* v. *Levinstein* (1883)).

In bankruptcy proceedings, the following matters must be heard in public: public examinations, approvals of compositions or schemes; discharge applications; applications for committal to prison for contempt, or for the trial of issues of fact by a jury, or for leave to participate in running a company; and appeals against rejections of proofs of debt where the amount exceeds £200 (*Bankruptcy Rules* 1952, *r.* 8).

There is no right of admission to creditors' meetings. The common practice is for the Official Receiver to ask creditors whether they object to the presence of the press, and to admit the press only if *no one* objects. A similar procedure applies to a meeting of a company's creditors where a winding-up order has been made.

12. Queen's Bench Division. Summonses (i.e. proceedings before a master or before a judge in chambers preliminary to the hearing of an action) are heard in chambers. Applications for interlocutory injunctions are also heard by the judge in chambers—whose jurisdiction also includes, e.g., the hearing of bail applications by persons remanded in custody. The entire proceedings, including the making of the order, are in chambers, but there is usually nothing to stop reporters obtaining information from the parties afterwards (subject to some exceptions: *see* VI, **17** and **18**).

An anomaly occurs in applications under Order 113, *Rules of the Supreme Court*, for possession of property (e.g. to evict squatters). They are heard in chambers if brought in the Q.B. Division, but in open court in the Chancery Division.

Where assessment of damages is adjourned to a High Court master or Official Referee, this is a "public proceeding" (*Hesz* v. *Sotheby & Co.* (1960)).

13. Family Division. Hearings of petitions for divorce, judicial separation, and nullity of marriage must (subject to *s.* 48(2) *Matrimonial Causes Act* 1973—below) be heard in open court (*Matrimonial Causes Rules* 1971, *r.* 37).

In *Scott* v. *Scott* (1913) the House of Lords rejected a contention that a nullity petition could be heard *in camera* in the interests of public decency, though the court could sit *in camera* if the administration of justice would be rendered impracticable by the presence of the public. (The Law Lords' speeches applied the same reasoning to any judicial proceeding.)

In *McPherson* v. *McPherson* (1936), a judge heard a divorce case in his lunch hour in the judges' library, with a "Private" notice on the door, but announced at the start of the hearing: "I am sitting in open court." HELD: the public could have had no suspicion that justice was being administered there; decisions reached in such circumstances could be set aside.

(*a*) *Injunctions.* In 1974 the President of the Family Division issued a Practice Direction that hearings of motions for interlocutory injunctions in that Division shall in future be in chambers unless the judge directs that for special reasons the hearing shall be in open court.

These are cases where a petitioner for divorce seeks an order of the court to restrain the other spouse from assaults or molestation, or perhaps to exclude the other spouse from the matrimonial home, pending the hearing of the divorce petition; or where one party seeks to restrain the other from removing a child of the family, or seeks an order for the return of a child who has been "snatched" or an injunction to prevent a husband transferring money out of the country so as to deprive his wife of maintenance.

Where, however, it is sought to commit a spouse to prison for breach of an injunction, the hearing must be in open court.

Under the *Matrimonial Causes Rules* 1968–73, the President's direction applies in county courts when they are exercising divorce jurisdiction.

(*b*) *Nullity petitions.* A decree nisi of nullity is a declaration by the court that a purported marriage is invalid. It may be void on the ground that, e.g., one of the parties was under age at the time of the ceremony, or was already married; or voidable on the ground of, e.g., the other spouse's wilful refusal or incapacity to consummate the marriage.

In the latter case it is necessary to adduce evidence of

attempts at intercourse. Section 48(2), *Matrimonial Causes Act* 1973, provides:

"In any proceedings for nullity of marriage, evidence on the question of sexual capacity shall be heard *in camera* unless in any case the judge is satisfied that in the interests of justice such evidence ought to be given in open court."

Note that it is only evidence of sexual capacity—not the entire proceeding—which may be taken *in camera*.

(*c*) *Guardianship and wardship.* Wardship proceedings— i.e. those relating to a person under 18 who is, or whom it is sought to make, a ward of court—are almost invariably in private, though the court occasionally seeks the assistance of the press. Order 90, *r.* 7, *Rules of Supreme Court*, empowers the High Court to hear *all* applications under the *Guardianship of Minors Act* 1971—including (*r.* 5) those relating to wards of court—in private.

(*d*) *Legitimacy declarations.* The *Matrimonial Causes Act* 1973, *s.* 45 (dealing with declarations of legitimacy) states: "The court . . . may direct that the whole or any part of the proceedings shall be heard *in camera*, and an application for a direction under this subsection shall be heard *in camera* unless the court otherwise directs." The question whether a child is a child of the family, must, however, be heard in open court (*Prior* v. *Prior* (1970)).

14. The Crown Court. The *Scott* v. *Scott* principles apply (*see* **1–3**). Except as laid down by the House of Lords in that case, or by statute (e.g. Official Secrets Acts), reporters cannot be excluded from Crown Court proceedings. Certain procedural matters (e.g. applications relating to legal aid) may be in chambers (*Crown Court Rules* 1971, *r.* 8), but an application for a change of venue for a Crown Court trial must be in open court (*Courts Act* 1971, *s.* 7(3)).

Searching of journalists (e.g. at terrorist trials) is without statutory power, but if the practice were challenged in the courts the criterion of "interests of the state" (*see* XI, **4**) might well be adopted.

PROCEEDINGS BEFORE MAGISTRATES

15. Magistrates' courts: criminal proceedings. These, whether summary or committal, must be heard in open court (except that in committal proceedings under the Official Secrets Acts certain evidence may be taken *in camera* before examining justices just as on indictment (*s.* 8(4), *Official Secrets Act* 1920)). (*See* also *s.* 6, *Criminal Justice Act* 1967, below.)

In 1971, reporters were excluded by police from a remand hearing before Coleshill, Warwickshire, magistrates, at which evidence of arrest was given against a girl of fourteen charged with murder. Afterwards, the police apologised: reporters were entitled to attend. All the magistrates could do—as they did in this case to an empty press bench—was to give a direction that nothing be published that would identify the girl. The proceedings being before an adult court, since juvenile courts cannot deal with cases of homicide, the restrictions applicable to reports of juvenile court proceedings (*see* X, **14**) did not apply.

Arbitrary exclusion of the press by magistrates during committal proceedings (e.g. at Worksop in 1960, when the accused included a number of local dignitaries, and at Bournemouth in 1962, when the charges involved alleged prostitution of teenaged girls) were partly remedied by *s.* 6, *Criminal Justice Act* 1967:

> "Examining justices shall sit in open court except where any enactment contains an express provision to the contrary, and except where it appears to them as respects the whole or any part of the committal proceedings that the ends of justice would not be served by their sitting in open court."

In 1948, a chief constable instructed his officers not to permit reporters to enter or leave a court room during the hearing of cases. Questioned in Parliament, the Home Secretary replied: "The Chief Constable carried out what he thought were the wishes of the Bench, and they subsequently came to the conclusion that it was not necessary for the steps to be taken."

16. Magistrates: licensing proceedings. At their general annual licensing meeting, the licensing authority must sit in public and, subject to the giving of proper notice, listen **to** objections (*Boulter* v. *Kent Justices* (1897)).

This applies also to betting and gaming licensing committees

(*Betting, Gaming and Lotteries Act* 1963, *s.* 1; *Gaming Act* 1968, *s.* 2).

17. Magistrates' courts: domestic proceedings. In 1946, a Mr. A. Garlick, a reporter at Cannock, was asked to leave the court because domestic proceedings were about to begin. He protested that he had a legal right to remain, and would institute High Court proceedings if removed by force. On conferring with their clerk, the Bench conceded that Mr. Garlick was right.

The right of the press to attend domestic proceedings is now contained in *s.* 57(2) *Magistrates' Courts Act* 1952, which provides that during such proceedings the only persons present shall be officers of the court, the parties, solicitors and counsel, and others concerned in the case or present at the invitation of either party, *representatives of newspapers and news agencies*, and any other person whom the court may permit to be present.

But *s.* 57(3) states:

> "When hearing domestic proceedings, a magistrates court may, if it thinks it necessary in the interests of the administration of justice or of public decency, direct that any persons not being officers of the court or parties to the case, the parties' solicitors or counsel, or other persons directly concerned in the case, be excluded during the taking of any indecent evidence."

NOTE:
- (*i*) *Stone's Justices' Manual*, 108th Edn., concludes: "This provision is wide enough to empower the exclusion of representatives of newspapers and press agencies."
- (*ii*) The power of exclusion applies only during the taking of indecent evidence, except that . . .
- (*iii*) *s.* 57(4) provides that where the parties to the domestic proceeding are also parties to proceedings for enforcing, e.g., maintenance or guardianship orders, and the proceedings are heard together, the above provisions shall apply to the whole proceedings "unless the court otherwise determines".
- (*iv*) The *Magistrates' Courts Act* 1952, *s.* 56, as amended, defines "domestic proceedings" as proceedings under the *Guardianship of Minors Acts* 1971 and 1973; the *Matrimonial Proceedings (Magistrates' Courts) Act* 1960; *ss.* 3 and 4, *Maintenance Orders (Facilities for Enforcement) Act* 1920; *s.* 4(3) *Family Allowances Act* 1965; or applications for consent to marriage. "Domestic Proceedings" also

include the hearing of application for an affiliation order (*Affiliation Proceedings* (*Amendment*) *Act* 1972, *s.* 3).

In 1952 reporters were excluded from Bromley (Kent) magistrates court during the hearing of an application by a girl of 18 for consent to marriage. There were howls of protest. The position is now covered expressly by the *Magistrates' Courts* (*Guardianship of Minors*) *Rules* 1974, *r.* 6:

"If a court which hears an application [for consent to marriage] considers it expedient in the interests of the minor, it may decide to hear the proceedings *in camera.*"

18. Admission to juvenile courts. (*See* also the *Windsor Express* case, 4). The *Children and Young Persons Act* 1933, *s.* 47(2) states:

". . . no person shall be present at any sitting of a juvenile court except: members and officers of the court; parties to the case before the court, their solicitors and counsel, and witnesses and other persons directly concerned in the case; bona fide representatives of newspapers and news agencies; and such other persons as the court may specially authorise to be present."

This right of admission does not apply when the court is dealing with fostering (*Children Act* 1958, *s.* 10) or the supervision of children awaiting adoption (*Adoption Act* 1958, Pt. IV, *s.* 47) or adoption applications themselves (*Children Act* 1975 *s.* 21(3)).

OTHER COURTS AND TRIBUNALS

19. Admission to coroners' courts. *Coroners' Rules* 1953, *r.* 14:

"Every inquest should be held in public: provided that the coroner may direct that the public be excluded from an inquest or part of an inquest if he considers that it would be in the interests of national security to do so".

In 1969, a coroner who conducted two inquests at hospitals directed that, "for certain special reasons of a medical nature not affecting the hospitals in any way", the inquests should be kept as quiet as possible and the press not informed. He admitted afterwards that he had mistakenly broken the rules.

The same rules (*r.* 15) prohibit the holding of an inquest on a

Sunday or (except in case of emergency) on Christmas Day, Good Friday or bank holidays.

20. Restrictive Practices Court. "The court may sit . . . either in private or in open court" (*Restrictive Trade Practices Act* 1956, Sch., para. 3).

21. Courts martial. Courts martial must sit, and give their findings and order, in public; except that a naval court martial may exclude the public as may a civilian court, and may do so to avoid disclosure of information which may be directly or indirectly useful to an enemy (*Naval Discipline Act* 1967, *s.* 61). Other courts martial may do so on a similar ground, or where "necessary or expedient in the interests of the administration of justice" (*Army Act* 1955, *s.* 94; *Air Force Act* 1955, *s.* 94).

Deliberations on findings or sentence must in all cases be in private, as must, in Army and R.A.F. courts martial, deliberations on any other matter.

22. County courts. The rules applicable to High Court proceedings apply also to county courts (*County Courts Act* 1959, *s.* 103). A county court *must* sit in private when dealing with adoption matters (*Children Act* 1975, *s.* 21(2)). It *may* sit in private: when hearing evidence in defended medical nullity petitions (*see* **18**, above); when considering ancillary matters such as maintenance, custody, etc. (*County Court Rules* 1953, Order 45a); in guardianship cases (*County Court Rules* 1963, Order 46); in legitimacy cases (*see* **9** above); and in applications under the *Rent Act* 1968 or the *Housing Act* 1969 (*Rent (County Court) Proceedings Rules* 1970).

The *Matrimonial Causes Rules* 1973, *r.* 48, provide a special procedure in undefended divorce cases based on the spouses' living apart, where there are no young children. The evidence is sifted in private (but may be inspected later.) The decree must be pronounced in open court.

23. Valuation courts. These, hearing proposals for amendments to rateable values, must sit in public unless satisfied that a party's interests would thereby be prejudiced (*Local Government Act* 1948, *s.* 48).

24. Tribunals. The Lands Tribunal must sit in public except when arbitrating under a reference by consent (*Lands Tribunal*

Rules 1975, *r.* 33). The Transport Tribunal must sit in public except during interlocutory appeals or argument on preliminary points of law (*Transport Tribunal Rules* 1965, *r.* 23).

Industrial tribunals may sit in private where national security so requires, or where evidence is likely to contain information the disclosure of which would violate a statute or a confidence, or seriously prejudice an employer's interests otherwise than in negotiations over terms and conditions of work, etc. (*Industrial Tribunals* (*Labour Relations*) *Regulations* 1975, *r.* 6). The same applies to the Employment Appeals Tribunal (*Employment Protection Act* 1975, Sch. 6).

Various rules govern other tribunals, e.g. a Medical Appeal Tribunal must sit in public unless there are "special reasons" to the contrary (*Industrial Injuries* (*Determination of Claims and Questions*) *Regulations* 1967). Similar provisions apply to National Insurance and Social Security tribunals, and appeals from any of these to the Commissioner. Some tribunals must sit in private if anyone involved in the proceedings so requests (e.g. *Electricity* (*Compulsory Wayleaves*) (*Hearing Procedure*) *Rules* 1967). Traffic Commissioners must hear road service licence applications in public, and may sit in public for any other purpose (*Road Traffic Act* 1960, *s.* 153).

Statutory instruments governing the multifarious tribunals may be traced through the *Index to Government Orders*, published biennially by H.M.S.O.

Appeals to the High Court on points of law are in public.

25. Tribunals of inquiry. These, set up by resolution of both Houses of Parliament (*see* VI, **29**) must sit in public unless of opinion that "it is in the public interest inexpedient to do so for reasons connected with the subject matter of the inquiry or the nature of the evidence to be given" (*Tribunals of Inquiry* (*Evidence*) *Act* 1921, *s.* 2).

26. Accident inquiries.

(*a*) *Rail*. An inquiry ordered by the Department of Trade into a rail accident shall be conducted in open court in such manner as may be thought most effectual for ascertaining the cause and circumstances of the accident (*Regulation of Railways Act* 1871, *s.* 7).

(*b*) *Air*. "The court shall hold the inquiry in open court save to the extent that the court is of opinion that, in the interests of justice or in the public interests, any part of the evidence, or any argument relating thereto, should be heard *in camera*" (*Civil Aviation* (*Investigation of Accidents*) *Regulations* 1969). An inspector's investigation is, however, in private.

(*c*) *Sea.* Inquiries into death and other casualties must generally be in public, but decisions—unless involving cancellation of an officer's certificate—may be given in writing to the parties (*Shipping Casualties and Appeals and Rehearings Rules* 1923).

27. Professional disciplinary inquiries.

(*a*) *Barristers.* Proceedings are in private unless the accused requests otherwise. Sentences of disbarment or suspension are published, other sentences may be. The same principles apply to an appeal to a panel of judges.

(*b*) *Solicitors.* Proceedings are in private. Findings and order must be given in public (*Solicitors* (*Disciplinary Proceedings*) *Rules* 1975, *r.* 24).

(*c*) *Doctors, dentists, opticians.* Disciplinary Committee must sit in public, but have power to deliberate *in camera* "at any time and for any purpose". Decisions must be given in public (*General Medical Council Disciplinary Committee* (*Procedure*) *Rules* 1970; *General Dental Council Disciplinary Committee* (*Procedure*) *Rules* 1957; *General Optical Council Disciplinary Committee* (*Procedure*) *Order* 1969).

(*d*) *Pharmacists.* Proceedings must open in public, but may continue in private. Decision must be given in public (*Pharmaceutical Society* (*Statutory Committee*) *Order* 1957).

(*e*) *Veterinary surgeons.* Disciplinary Committee must sit in public except if of opinion that the interests of justice require exclusion of the public for any part of the proceedings. Decisions must be given in public (*Veterinary Surgeons and Veterinary Practitioners* (*Procedure and Evidence*) *Rules* 1967).

(*f*) *Clergy.* Consistory court may, during any part of proceedings, exclude such persons as it sees fit if satisfied that this is in the interests of justice. Decisions must be given in public.

NOTE: Appeals to the High Court or Judicial Committee of the Privy Council are in public.

28. Public inquiries. Inquiries into various plans under the *Community Land Act* 1975 must be in public (*ss.* 2(2) and 55), as must inquiries under various other enactments, e.g. *Land Compensation Act* 1961, *s.* 2(2). Though some statutes refer to "local inquiry" and others to "*public* local inquiry", the public are generally in fact admitted. The requirements as to public notice would seem otiose if there were no public right of admission.

29. Press accommodation. A right to attend proceedings does not confer a right to any special accommodation. The N.U.J. protested when reporters were excluded from the press bench at Winchester Crown Court, and had to sit at the back of the court where hearing was difficult, during a trial involving numerous defendants represented by even more numerous lawyers. The Lord Chancellor's Department replied, apologetically, that this step was "unavoidable".

In 1973 the journal of the Magistrates Association urged that the press bench should be equally sacrosanct as that of the magistrates.

PROGRESS TEST 9

1. In what circumstances may courts sit in private? **(2)**

2. What happened in the *Windsor Express* case? **(4)**

3. What evidence may be taken *in camera* in a nullity petition? **(13)**

4. Can reporters be excluded from (*a*) committal proceedings, (*b*) domestic proceedings before magistrates, (*c*) coroners' courts? **(15, 17, 19)**

5. Have reporters a right to attend proceedings before a licensing authority? **(16)**

6. May reporters attend juvenile court proceedings? Are there any circumstances in which they may be excluded? **(18, 4)**

7. May reporters be excluded from courts martial? **(21)**

8. In what circumstances may county courts sit in private? **(22)**

9. Must (*a*) valuation courts, and (*b*) tribunals of inquiry, sit in public? **(23, 25)**

10. Explain reporters' admission rights to (*a*) rail, and (*b*) air accident inquiries. **(26)**

11. Have reporters a right to sit in the press bench? **(29)**

CHAPTER X

RESTRICTIONS ON COURT REPORTING

WHERE THE LAW INTERVENES

1. Explanation. Although a reporter may have a right of admission to a court, there are instances where what he may report is restricted. Reports of committal proceedings in criminal cases are severely restricted by the *Criminal Justice Act* 1967; those of juvenile court proceedings by the *Children and Young Persons Acts* 1933 and 1969; those of domestic proceedings before magistrates' courts by the *Magistrates' Courts Act* 1952 and amending Acts; and those of divorce, judicial separation and nullity proceedings by the *Judicial Proceedings* (*Regulation of Reports*) *Act* 1926. This last Act also makes it an offence to report indecent details from *any* proceedings (*see* **16** below).

COMMITTAL PROCEEDINGS

2. Reporting restrictions. Section 3, *Criminal Justice Act* 1967, restricts reports of committal proceedings in magistrates' courts. Section 3(4) provides that a report of committal proceedings may contain only:

(*a*) the identity of the court and the names of the examining justices;

(*b*) the names, addresses and occupations of the parties and witnesses, and the ages of the defendant or defendants and witnesses;

(*c*) the offence or offences, or a summary of them, with which the defendant or defendants is or are charged;

(*d*) the names of counsel and solicitors engaged in the proceedings;

(*e*) any decision of the court to commit the defendant or any of the defendants for trial, and any decision of the court on the disposal of the case of any defendants not committed;

(*f*) where the court commits the defendant or any of the

defendants for trial, the charge or charges, or a summary of them, on which he is committed;

(*g*) where the committal proceedings are adjourned, the date and place to which they are adjourned;

(*h*) any arrangements as to bail on committal or adjournment;

(*i*) whether legal aid was granted to the defendant or any of the defendants.

3. Prosecutions under s. 3. In 1973 the publishers and editor of a newspaper were fined over a report of committal proceedings on an indecency charge. The headline described the accused as a "New Year's Day Bridegroom", and the report described him as "bespectacled and dressed in a dark suit", set out the date and place of his marriage, described the charge as "serious", and referred to the prosecution submitting "original statements and exhibits".

This was a decision of magistrates only. If the newspaper had appealed, the decision might well have been reversed.

In 1975 a former editor of another newspaper was fined over a report which included details of the effects of fires which the accused, on charges of arson, was alleged to have started. If the information had come from extraneous sources—not what was said in court—there would have been no offence under *s.* 3 (though there may have been a contempt).

4. Lifting of restrictions. The accused, or his lawyer, may seek an order lifting the restrictions. Such an application must be granted. Section 3(2) states:

"A magistrates court *shall*, on an application . . . by the defendant or one of the defendants, order that the foregoing subsection [i.e. the reporting restrictions] shall not apply to reports of those proceedings".

Where one of a number of co-defendants opts for full publicity, the entire proceedings may be reported, even though it is against the wishes of the other defendants. Thus a stipendiary magistrate acted wrongly in confining his "lifting" order to those defendants who asked for it (*R.* v. *Russell, ex parte Beaverbrook Newspapers Ltd.* (1969)). "If one defendant obtains an order, all the other defendants involved are also subject to the full glare of publicity which used to apply before the Act was passed"—Lord Widgery.

Similarly, if one person subsequently becomes a defendant in committal proceedings in which reporting restrictions have already been lifted, he is bound by the "lifting". In *R.* v. *Blackpool Justices, ex parte Beaverbrook Newspapers Ltd.* (1972), nine people had appeared in committal proceedings, and some had opted for publicity. A tenth—Sewell—was later arrested and charged: it was held that Sewell had to "fall into line".

An accused person may apply for a "lifting" order before the committal proceedings proper have begun (*R.* v. *Bow Street Magistrate, ex parte Reginald Kray* (1968)).

The defendant must be informed of his right to apply for a waiver of the restrictions on publicity (*Magistrates' Courts Rules* 1968, *r.* 2(1)).

Where the court has made an order removing the restrictions, it should announce at the beginning of any adjourned hearing that such an order has been made (*r.* 2(3)).

5. If the accused is not committed. It is not unlawful under the Act to publish or broadcast a report of committal proceedings after the magistrates have decided not to commit the defendant for trial (*s.* 3(3)(*a*)). But if there is more than one defendant, it applies only if none of the defendants are committed for trial.

6. After the trial. Section 3(3)(*b*) provides that if the court commits the defendant or any of the defendants for trial, it is not unlawful under the Act to publish or broadcast matter—which would otherwise be prohibited—from the committal proceedings after the conclusion of the trial or, if there is more than one defendant, the trial of the last to be tried.

> NOTE: a report in the circumstances of either **5** or **6** above is deemed to be "contemporaneous" within the meaning of the *Law of Libel Amendment Act* 1888, *s.* 3 (*see* II, **11**) if published as soon as practicable after it becomes lawful to do so (*Criminal Justice Act* 1967, *s.* 5).

7. Indictable offences tried summarily. Some offences (e.g. murder) are indictable offences only, and may be tried only on indictment before the Crown Court; other offences (e.g. parking) are summary offences, and may be dealt with only by magistrates. In between are offences which may be tried either on indictment or summarily before magistrates.

Section 3(3) goes on to deal with the situation where, in

committal proceedings for such offences, a court proceeds to deal with one or more of the defendants summarily, while committing the other defendant(s) for trial. It provides that, in such a situation, "it shall not be unlawful under this section to publish or broadcast, as part of the report of the summary trial . . . a report of so much of the committal proceedings containing any such matter [i.e. "prohibited" matter] as takes place before the determination" [i.e. the decision to try one of more of the defendants summarily].

8. When restrictions are lifted. When restrictions are lifted, or otherwise cease to apply, reporters may find little to report. Sections 1 and 2 of the Act enable written statements to be put in instead of oral evidence, where the defence consents. They are not available to the press, and not read out.

In proceedings at Stafford for cat stealing, the "evidence" consisted of written statements and seventeen cats. The accused's solicitor, having obtained a "lifting" order to attract potential witnesses, found his purpose defeated by *s*. 1.

NOTE: the name and address of the maker of a written statement should be read out unless the court otherwise directs— *Magistrates' Courts Rules* 1968, *r*. 58(6).

DIVORCE AND ANCILLARY PROCEEDINGS

9. Reporting restrictions. *Judicial Proceedings* (*Regulation of Reports*) *Act* 1926, *s*. 1(1):

"It shall not be lawful to print or publish, or cause or procure to be printed or published . . . (*b*) in relation to a judicial proceeding for dissolution of marriage, for nullity of marriage, for judicial separation . . . any particulars other than the following . . . (*i*) the names, addresses and occupations [NOTE: not the ages] of the parties and witnesses; (*ii*) a concise statement of the charges, defences and counter-charges in support of which evidence has been given; (*iii*) submissions on any point of law arising in the proceedings, and the decision of the court thereon; (*iv*) the . . . judgment of the court, and observations made by the court in giving judgment".

The *Domestic and Appellate Proceedings* (*Restriction of Publicity*) *Act* 1968, *s*. 2, as amended by the *Matrimonial Causes Act* 1973, extends the above restrictions to proceedings under the 1973 Act for:

(*a*) a declaration of legitimacy, or

(*b*) financial provision for a spouse.

10. Proceedings for infringement. Penalty (1926 Act, *s.* 1(2)): imprisonment not exceeding four months, a fine not exceeding £500, or both; "provided that no person other than a proprietor, editor, master printer or publisher shall be liable to be convicted under this Act". Prosecution requires leave of the Attorney-General (*s.* 1(3)).

The restrictions (including that in **16**) do not apply to law reports not forming part of any other publication, or to legal or medical technical journals (*s.* 1(4)).

In *Duchess of Argyll* v. *Duke of Argyll* (1967) an injunction was granted to restrain publication of details which had emerged in the Duke's divorce suit against the Duchess, partly because publication would have infringed the 1926 Act.

NOTE: appeals to the High Court or Court of Appeal on domestic or ancillary matrimonial matters are generally listed by initials only, and to identify the parties would be a contempt.

11. Magistrates' courts: domestic proceedings. The *Magistrates' Courts Act* 1952, *s.* 58, limits what may be reported to the particulars set out in the 1926 Act in **9** above.

12. Proceedings for infringement. These are as in **10**, except that the maximum fine is £100, and the 1952 Act contains no reference to "master printer".

PROCEEDINGS INVOLVING CHILDREN

13. Reporting restrictions. The *Children and YoungPersons Act* 1933, *s.* 49(1):

". . . no newspaper report of any proceedings in a juvenile court shall reveal the name, address or school, or include any particulars calculated to lead to the identification, of any child or young person concerned in those proceedings, either as being the person against whom or in respect of whom the proceedings are taken, or as being a witness therein, nor shall any picture be published in any newspaper as being or including a picture of any child or young person so concerned in any such proceedings . . .

"Provided that the court or the Secretary of State may in any case, if satisfied that it is in the interests of justice so to do, by

order dispense with the requirements of this section to such
extent as may be specified in the order".

The *Children and Young Persons Act* 1969, *s*. 10, extended the
restriction so that the court or the Secretary of State may now
dispense with the requirements only if "it is appropriate to do
so for the purpose of avoiding injustice to a child or young
person" (e.g. to avoid confusion with an innocent child or young
person). No longer has the court power to permit identification
of a juvenile offender on the ground that it considers that the
offender deserves it.

The *Children and Young Persons Act* 1963, *s*. 57(4) extends
the restriction to sound and television broadcasts.

The maximum penalty is a £50 fine (1933 Act, *s*. 49(2)).

NOTE:
    (*i*) The restrictions do not apply where a juvenile appears in
        an adult court charged jointly with an adult, unless the
        court makes an order under *s*. 39 of the 1933 Act (*see* **14**);
        but editors usually show discretion.
    (*ii*) "conviction" and "sentence" must not be used in relation
        to juveniles (*s*. 59 of the 1933 Act).

Restrictions governing reports of juvenile court proceedings
apply also to any proceedings on appeal from a juvenile court
(*s*. 57 of the 1963 Act).

14. Court's power in any proceedings. Section 39 of the
1933 Act, as amended by *s*. 57(1) of the 1963 Act, states that in
relation to *any* proceedings in *any* court, the court may give a
direction prohibiting identification of any child or young person
by whom, against whom, or in respect of whom proceedings are
taken, in similar terms to those set out in **13** above.

The maximum penalty is a £50 fine.

Section 57(4) of the 1963 Act extends this restriction to
sound and television broadcasts.

In a case of incest where one of the participants is a minor,
one generally has the choice between identifying the accused
but describing the charge as, e.g., a sexual offence against a girl,
or describing the charge as incest but omitting to identify the
accused. The Press Council advocates the former.

15. Wardship proceedings. Judges of the High Court
Family Division are always careful to ensure that a ward of

court is not identified. Lord Justice Russell spelt out the warning in 1970 when dealing with an appeal involving a foster child who had been made a ward of court:

> "We decided to hear this appeal *in camera* with a view to protecting the infant from harm, and we now give judgment in open court, taking every care that we can to avoid identification of the persons concerned. No doubt diligent investigation would enable anyone interested to tear aside the veil. But . . . the infant is a ward of court . . . and if anyone is minded to question or interview the infant he may well be at risk of being in contempt."

MISCELLANEOUS RESTRICTIONS

16. Indecent details. The *Judicial Proceedings* (*Regulation of Reports*) *Act* 1926, *s*. 1(1) states:

> "It shall not be lawful to print or publish, or cause or procure to be printed or published, in relation to *any* judicial proceedings, any indecent matter, or indecent medical, surgical or physiological details, being matter or details the publication of which would be calculated to injure public morals."

17. Proceedings in chambers. Subject to the judge's powers, and other conditions (*see* VI, **17**), there is no restriction on interviewing parties when they emerge from a hearing in chambers—though obviously extreme care is needed where only one side is willing to talk. (No privilege attaches to such a report.)

To attempt to ascertain the purport of proceedings held *in camera* would be likely to give rise to contempt (*R*. v. *Prager*; *see* VI, **18**), and note the contempt in reporting a trial-within-a-trial (*see* VI, **14**) or the fact or amount of a payment into court (*see* VI, **19**).

18. Judges' powers. Lord Widgery's judgment in *R*. v. *Socialist Worker* (1974) (*see* VI, **21**) lends judicial support to the view that judges have a residual power to *order*, and not merely *request*, journalists not to identify certain witnesses. Lord Widgery said he was satisfied that the trial judge in that case gave a direction, and not a mere request, that the two principal prosecution witnesses in that case should be known only as Messrs. X and Y. He did not suggest that the judge had no such power, and the tenor of his judgment was to the contrary.

In a blackmail case in 1972 (*The Times*, July 18) Mr. Justice Caulfield said he could find "no legal authority" for ordering, as distinct from requesting, the press not to identify the victim.

The *Sexual Offences (Amendment) Act* 1976 prohibits identification, unless the court otherwise directs, of complainants (*s.* 4) or the accused (*s.* 6) in rape cases. The accused may be identified on conviction.

19. Magistrates' powers. Except as explained in **11**, **13** and **14**, magistrates are powerless to tell journalists what they may or may not publish. The Younger Committee (*see* XIII) recommended that magistrates should be readier to *ask* journalists not to identify offenders where identification might cause the offender or members of his family "a risk of severe mental disturbance". They suggested that non-compliance should be "a ground of complaint to the Press Council".

20. Rehabilitation of Offenders Act 1974. Section 9 makes it an offence for a person, e.g. a court official, who in the course of his duties has access to official records giving details of "spent" convictions, to make unauthorised disclosure of such information. No doubt the recipient of such information would be aiding and abetting the principal offence. Prosecution requires consent of the D.P.P.

Lord Widgery issued a Practice Direction in 1975 that "no one should refer to a spent conviction in open court without the consent of the judge", and spent convictions should not be read out as antecedents of offenders.

Even if the accused deprives himself of the usual protection against cross-examination as to his previous bad character, the court may now feel inhibited from allowing him to be asked about spent convictions (although the court has this power— *see* III, **3**).

21. Bankruptcy. Obviously, one cannot report an application for an order to stop the advertisement of a receiving order in bankruptcy unless and until the application is refused (*Bankruptcy Act* 1914, *s.* 11). Since it is open to any debtor to make such an application, reference should not be made to a bankruptcy petition or receiving order until the receiving order has been advertised in the *London Gazette*.

22. Orders for search of premises. Proceedings for an order enabling premises to be searched for, e.g., confidential or copyright material, may not be published unless the order is refused or, if it is granted, until after it has been executed.

23. Note of appeal, etc. Where a person found guilty of misconduct has a specified time (e.g. 14 days for solicitors under Order 106, *r.* 12, *Rules of the Supreme Court*, and 28 days under the *Medical Act* 1950 and the *Dentists Act* 1957) within which to lodge an appeal, or where the findings and order are subject to confirmation (e.g. in a court martial) the report should say so.

Where the Attorney-General, after an acquittal, refers a point of law for consideration by the Court of Appeal (Criminal Division) the acquitted person should not be identified (*Criminal Appeal (Reference of Points of Law) Rules* 1973.

PHOTOGRAPHS

24. Photographing persons involved in court proceedings. The *Criminal Justice Act* 1925, *s.* 41(1) states:

"No person shall (*a*) take or attempt to take in any court any photograph, or, with a view to publication, make or attempt to make in any court any portrait or sketch of any person, being a judge of the court, or a juror or a witness in, or a party to, any proceedings before the court, whether civil or criminal, or (*b*) publish any photograph, portrait or sketch taken or made in contravention of this section, or any reproduction thereof."

NOTE:

(*i*) "Court" includes a coroner's court (*s.* 41(2) (*a*)).

(*ii*) "Court" includes the court room, or the building or its precincts in which the court is held, and it is an offence to make a photograph, portrait or sketch of a person entering or leaving such court room, building or precincts (*s.* 41(2) (*c*)). "Precincts" has never been precisely delineated, but a photograph with a court building in the background would be likely to infringe the subsection. If the judge or magistrates take a view of the *locus in quo*, or take evidence in, e.g., a hospital, that place would, it is submitted, be "precincts".

(*iii*) "Judge" includes recorder, registrar, magistrate, justice or coroner.

PROGRESS TEST 10

1. What matters may be reported in any committal proceedings ? **(2)**

2. "Even innocuous details may infringe *s.* 3, *Criminal Justice Act* 1967"—Explain **(3)**

3. What is the position where one accused person wishes reporting restrictions to be lifted, but his co-accused does not ? **(4)**

4. What matters may be reported in divorce proceedings ? **(9)**

5. Do any restrictions apply to domestic proceedings before magistrates ? **(11)**

6. What restrictions apply to reports of (*a*) juvenile court proceedings (*b*) appeals from such proceedings ? **(13)**

7. Do (*a*) judges, and (*b*) magistrates, have any power to give reporters directions as to what may or may not be published ? **(18, 19)**

8. How may the *Rehabilitation of Offenders Act* 1974 impede court journalists ? **(20)**

9. Explain the provisions governing the taking of photographs outside courts. **(24)**

10. What does the word "court" include ? **(24)**

CHAPTER XI

JOURNALISTS' SOURCES

1. Explanation. A cardinal rule is that a journalist does not divulge sources of information. Many informants would "dry up" if not confident that their identities would be kept secret.

But the rules of evidence do not give journalists a privilege (i.e. a right to refuse to answer certain questions in evidence) as they do in some circumstances to, e.g., lawyers. The professional rule cannot be elevated into a legal rule, said Lord Denning in *Attorney-General* v. *Mulholland and Foster* (1963).

2. Examples. In *Attorney-General* v. *Mulholland and Foster* (1963) journalists were imprisoned for refusing to identify their sources before the tribunal inquiring into the Vassall spy affair. In *Attorney-General* v. *Clough* (1963) a third journalist was sentenced for similarly refusing, but escaped his sentence when his source voluntarily came forward.

In 1975 Gordon Airs, of the *Daily Record*, was fined £500 for refusing to identify a source when called as a witness in a "Tartan Army" trial.

3. Power to demand sources. A journalist may be required to identify his sources before courts, tribunals of inquiry (*see* VI, **29**), or a Committee of either House of Parliament (*see* VII). In the Allighan affair (*see* VII, **3**) the *Evening News* editor was held to be in contempt for refusing to tell the Committee of Privileges which M.P. had been writing a political column in his newspaper. No action was taken against him, nor against Mr. Gordon Greig of the *Daily Mail* when he withheld a source from the Committee (*see* VII, **5**).

4. Judicial attitudes. Some courts adopt an authoritarian approach. Lord Emslie said in the Gordon Airs case (*see* **2**, above): "Any witness, including any journalist witness, who declines to answer any competent and relevant question in court, must realise that he will be in contempt and liable to incur severe punishment".

In Clough's case (*see* **2**) Lord Parker told Clough: "There must be emergencies in the interests of the state where private interests, professional interests and all interests must be subordinated. Your informant himself is under a duty to come forward and assist the interests of the state. How can you say that there is any dishonour on you if you do what is your duty as a citizen to put the interests of the state above everything?"

NOTE: the "interests of the state" was adopted as a criterion in *Elias* v. *Pasmore* (1934)—a much criticised decision: see, e.g., Street, *Freedom, the Individual and the Law*.

Lord Parker said: "The courts, so far as they have been involved, have been sympathetic" to the position of journalists. When, however, he was chairman of the Bank Rate Tribunal in 1957, two City editors were reluctant to identify their sources, but did so when *directed*.

Mr. Justice James, when chairman of the tribunal investigating the collapse of the Vehicle & General Insurance Co., declined to press a *Sunday Times* journalist to reveal how he knew that a Department of Trade inspector had been pressing for action for two years before the company's collapse. The judge said: "We do not think this is a case where the witness should be asked or pressed to go contrary to his belief as a member of his profession."

Less indulgence is likely to be shown where an editor declines merely to name the reporter who wrote a story, as distinct from the reporter's source. Alan Hitchins, editor of the *South London Advertiser*, when called as a witness at the Old Bailey in 1956, was asked to identify the reporter who wrote a story. He refused, "in view of newspaper practice". Judge Maude replied: "Of giving away your informants, I know that. Isn't this rather different?" Mr. Hitchins named the reporter (*Manchester Guardian*, 22nd September 1956).

5. No general duty of disclosure. Except as set out in **3** and **6**, a journalist cannot be required to disclose his source.

In 1963, Brierley Hill U.D.C.'s Finance Committee demanded to know the names of a newspaper's reporter and his informant responsible for a story giving advance information about a proposed increase in the local rate. The paper's editor said he had "not the slightest intention" of telling them.

In 1958, the dominant Labour group on Glasgow Corporation

were minded to take some action (unspecified) against a city journalist who published details contained in a confidential document about proposed increases in council house rents, and against his informant. They were powerless to do anything about the former, and unable to ascertain the latter.

In 1959, Nottingham Branch of the N.U.J. complained to the Press Council about visits to the *Nottingham Evening Post* by C.I.D. officers demanding to know the identities of the writers of certain nom-de-plume letters to the editor. The Press Council adjudicated: "The police must be at liberty to make inquiries in newspaper offices as elsewhere, but it was improper for a request to be made to a journalist to become a source of supply for general information on security matters."

6. Official Secrets Act 1920, s. 6. One instance where statute requires disclosure is under *s*. 6, Official Secrets Act 1920:

> "It shall be the duty of every person to give on demand to a chief officer of police, or to a superintendent or other officer of police not below the rank of inspector appointed by a chief officer for the purpose . . . any information in his power relating to an offence or a suspected offence under the [*Official Secrets Act* 1911] . . . and if any person fails to give such information . . . he shall be guilty of an offence".

In *Lewis* v. *Cattle* (1938) Ernest Lewis, a *Daily Dispatch* journalist, wrote a story about a wanted man, the information for which could have come only from a police officer, whose identity the police wished to know. Lewis refused to tell them. Magistrates convicted him. Rejecting his appeal, the Lord Chief Justice said the case was "too plain for argument".

7. Demands are rare. In the Parliamentary furore which followed the *Mulholland and Foster* case (*see* **2**) the Attorney-General said: "The occasions when a journalist can be required to disclose the identity of his informant are extremely rare, and do not in practice arise in the ordinary courts. They occur only when it becomes important for a tribunal or a committee of either House of Parliament to inquire into the truth of an allegation made by a journalist."

He said the number of times a journalist had been required to divulge his source in the preceding eighty years was "about six".

8. Theft of a document: R. v. May (1975). David May, a journalist, obtained photographs of a Spanish banker after the banker's kidnap in Paris in 1974. The photographs, to prove their authenticity, were accompanied by the banker's Paris residence permit. May refused to tell police the source of the photographs and permit. He was charged with handling stolen property (the permit) but was acquitted.

The prosecution admitted that he would not have been charged if he had disclosed his source. They maintained that the journalists' code of conduct was overridden because the banker's life was at stake. The judge said the journalists' code of silence was "not inflexible", and "there may be circumstances in which . . . it is more honourable to preserve life than a confidence".

9. Theft of a document: the Railway Gazette. In 1973, the *Sunday Times* and the *Railway Gazette* published stories about projected cuts in rail services, based on a confidential document which officials alleged had been "removed" from Ministry offices. Police raided the offices of the *Railway Gazette*, saying they were investigating an alleged "theft" of the document—but failed to find the source through which it had been leaked. The Attorney-General later felt there was "insufficient information" on which to charge anyone with "stealing" a *photocopy* of the document.

A threatened prosecution of Harold Evans, editor of the *Sunday Times*, under the Official Secrets Acts, also came to nought (*see* XVI, 7).

What one M.P. called "a monstrous and sinister witchhunt on the press" was said by Mr. Heath, then Prime Minister, to be "entirely a police matter".

10. Sources when a newspaper is sued. In interlocutory proceedings (i.e. proceedings preparatory to the hearing of a civil action) an interrogatory cannot generally be served requiring a newspaper, when sued for libel, to reveal its source. (Interrogatories are questions by one party which the other party is required to answer on oath.) In *Lyon* v. *Daily Telegraph* (1943) it was held that a newspaper could not be required to reveal its source where fair comment was pleaded. In *Lawson* v. *Odhams Press Ltd.* (1949) the Court of Appeal would not allow a sports writer to be required to reveal his source where justification was pleaded.

These decisions are now embodied in the *Rules of the Supreme Court.*

In 1976 a judge refused to order a newspaper to reveal its source of information to a former Government minister who was suing the newspaper publishers for alleged infringement of copyright and misuse of confidential information (*Brayley* v. *Associated Newspapers Ltd.* (1976)).

11. Possible changes. The promised repeal of *s.* 2, *Official Secrets Act* 1911 (*see* XVI, **9**) would mean a journalist would commit no offence such as in *Lewis* v. *Cattle* (*see* **6**) if the information in question were such as might infringe *s.* 2, but not *s.* 1, of the 1911 Act.

Questioned in Parliament after the *Mulholland* case, the Attorney-General said: "I can hold out no hope of amending legislation"; and later: "It must be remembered that every time an individual, be he a journalist or anyone else, is entitled not to tell the whole truth, innocent third parties may get less than justice".

Lord Shawcross, who later became chairman of the Press Council, said in evidence before the Salmon Committee (*see* VI, **29**): "My experience is that a journalist is very rarely asked to disclose a source unless it is absolutely necessary. If that is the view of the judge, or of an inquiry tribunal, I think the source ought to be disclosed, and that the public interest in knowing the source must prevail".

PROGRESS TEST 11

1. What is the meaning of "privilege" in relation to the giving of evidence ? **(1)**

2. Which bodies have power to require a journalist to reveal a source of information ? What powers have they in case of a refusal ? **(2, 3, 4).**

3. Can a local authority demand to know a journalist's souce of information ? **(5)**

4. Can the police demand to know a journalist's source of information ? **(6, 7)**

5. Explain the decision in *Lewis* v. *Cattle*. **(6)**

6. In what circumstances may a journalist who withholds a source of information be proceeded against under the *Theft Act* 1968 ? **(8, 9)**

7. What are "interrogatories" ? **(10)**

CHAPTER XII

OBSCENITY

WHAT IS "OBSCENE"?

1. Explanation. The law of obscenity exists to deter or punish the publication of matter which tends to deprave or corrupt those who are likely to read, see or hear it, or to corrupt public morals or outrage public decency.

2. The common law offence. In *R.* v. *Curl* (1727) the Attorney-General successfully argued: "This [obscene libel] is an offence at common law as it tends to corrupt the morals of the King's subjects and is against the peace of the King".

R. v. *Hicklin* (1868) laid down the test: "whether the tendency of the matter charged as obscene is to deprave and corrupt those whose minds are open to such immoral influences and into whose hands a publication of this sort may fall".

Decided cases before 1960 are based on this definition. The common law offence still survives, but in abeyance.

3. Obscene Publications Act 1959, s. 1. This has largely superseded the common law definition. It reads:

"An article shall be deemed to be obscene if its effect, or (where the article comprises two or more distinct items) the effect of one of its items, is, if taken as a whole, such as to tend to deprave and corrupt persons who are likely, having regard to all relevant circumstances, to read, see or hear the matter contained or embodied in it".

4. Definitions.

Article: "any description of article to be read, or looked at, or both; any sound record; any film or other record of a picture or pictures" (*s.* 1(2) *O.P.A.* 1959). The *O.P.A.* 1964, *s.* 2, extends the definition to anything intended for the reproduction of obscene articles – e.g. photographic negatives.

Publishing: A person "publishes" an article if he distributes,

circulates, sells, or lets it on hire, or gives or lends it or offers it
for sale or letting on hire; or, in the case of, e.g., a record or
film, plays or shows it (*O.P.A.* 1959, *s.* 1(3)). A proviso exempts
television and sound broadcasts, and certain cinematograph
exhibitions (see, e.g., *Attorney-General's Reference No. 2 of 1975*).

5. "Deprave and corrupt". It is not sufficient that the
article tends merely to *shock* the likely reader not to deprave
and corrupt him. In *R.* v. *Martin Secker & Warburg Ltd.* (1954)
—where *The Philanderer* was "acquitted"—Mr. Justice Stable
said the charge was not that the book tended to shock or
disgust. "That is not a criminal offence. The charge is that the
tendency of the book is to corrupt and deprave".

In the House of Lords in 1972, Lord Wilberforce said one
consequence of the 1959 Act appeared to be that an article was
not obscene if it merely *shocked* people, however many (*D.P.P.*
v. *Whyte* (1972)).

In *R.* v. *Penguin Books Ltd.* (1960)—where a jury "acquitted"
D. H. Lawrence's *Lady Chatterley's Lover*—Mr. Justice Byrne
defined "deprave and corrupt":

> "Deprave": "to make morally bad, to pervert, to debase, to
> corrupt morally".
> "Corrupt": "to render morally unsound or rotten, to destroy
> the moral purity or chastity, to pervert or ruin
> a good quality, to debase, to defile". (*The Times,*
> November 2nd, 1960).

6. Juries set the standards. The major obscenity trials
have been before juries (though proceedings under the Act may
be brought either summarily or on indictment). In an obscenity
trial in 1973, Mr. Justice Bristow told the jury: "You have to
decide whether the magazine went too far by today's standards
of decency. *You are the people who have to say what those standards
are.*"

In *The Philanderer* case (above) the judge told the jury that
their verdict would have "a great bearing upon where the line
is drawn between liberty, that freedom to read and think as the
spirit moves us on the one hand, and licence, which is an affront
to the society of which we are all members, on the other."

Juries' verdicts do not create precedents. Judges on appeal
decide questions on law, but the decision of jury A in relation

to one article does not bind jury B in relation to a similar—or even the same—article.

In *D.P.P.* v. *Staniforth* (1976) a judge said (when the case was in the Court of Appeal) that it was doubtful whether juries' verdicts in obscenity cases could maintain "any reasonable degree of consistency".

Judges have often stressed the desirability of jury trial in obscenity cases. In one case before a judge alone—Mr. Justice Bridge in 1973—he said: "I cannot help thinking that a jury is a better tribunal to decide this question [whether imported magazines depicting naked boys were obscene] than a judge alone" (*Commissioners of Customs and Excise* v. *Sun and Health Ltd.* (1973)).

7. Judicial attitudes. Juries are influenced by judicial attitudes. The summing-up in *The Philanderer* was hailed as enlightened. More recently, a recorder told a jury which had convicted publishers of homosexual magazines: "If you had decided these documents were not indecent, I should have lost my faith in juries." And a circuit judge observed: "The shrill petulant protest of licentious libertines has been resoundingly rejected."

In 1965, Lord Parker said of *Cain's Book* (*see* **12**): "The less said about it, the better."

TESTS FOR OBSCENITY

8. Test is contemporary standards. An article must be judged by the standards of today. What would have been adjudged obscene ten years ago may not be so today.

In *The Philanderer* case, the judge told the jury: "Your task is to decide whether you think the tendency of the book is to deprave those . . . into whose hands the book may fall *this year*.'

In *R.* v. *Calder & Boyers Ltd.* (1968)—where *Last Exit to Brooklyn* was "acquitted" on appeal—Lord Justice Salmon said: "The jury must set the standards of what is acceptable, or what is for the public good, *in the age in which we live*."

In a case in 1969, Mr. John Mortimer Q.C. submitted that the standards to be applied were "neither those of Mrs. Mary Whitehouse nor those of Mr. Kenneth Tynan".

9. "Persons who are likely . . . to read", etc., the article. In the *Last Exit* case, Lord Justice Salmon said the jury should have been directed to consider whether the effect of the book was to tend to deprave and corrupt "a significant proportion" of the persons likely to read it.

In *The Philanderer* case, the judge suggested that the standards should not be those of a 14-year-old schoolgirl. "A mass of literature—great literature—is, from many angles, wholly unsuitable for reading by the adolescent, but that does not mean that the publisher is guilty of a criminal offence for making those works available to the public."

An article in a newspaper is likely to be read by persons of varying ages and susceptibilities, so it would be futile to suggest that such an article was unlikely to be read by a given class of persons.

Most decided cases on this topic have concerned other types of publication. In *R.* v. *Will Barker* (1962) Mr. Justice Ashworth said "A person who sells potentially obscene matter to an unknown applicant takes the risk that the latter is someone whom the article would deprave and corrupt. On the other hand, if the unknown applicant is not of that type, the accused's ignorance of the applicant's character cannot make the article obscene."

In 1972 the House of Lords rejected an argument that obscene books had not been published to persons whom they would "tend to deprave or corrupt" because the only purchasers were men who were already so depraved as to be beyond corruption. The court should not decide who are the most likely readers, and then exclude all others from consideration (*D.P.P.* v. *Whyte* (1972).

10. Publisher's intention is irrelevant. In the *Last Exit* case, Lord Justice Salmon said: "However pure and noble the intent may have been [i.e. to shock the reader into doing what he could to eradicate the degradation of life in Brooklyn] if in fact the book, taken as a whole, tended to corrupt and deprave a significant proportion of those likely to read it, it was 'obscene' within the meaning of that word in the Act."

In the *Lady Chatterley* case (*see* 5) the judge would not permit the defence to call evidence that the author did not intend to deprave and corrupt (though a mass of expert evidence as to the book's *literary* merit was called, *see* 15).

In *R.* v. *Hicklin* (1868) an article was held to be obscene though the author's intention was not to injure public morals but to attack what he regarded as the iniquity of a particular religion.

In *Shaw* v. *D.P.P.* (1962) Lord Simonds said: ". . . the criminal character of the publication is not affected or qualified by there being some ulterior object in view . . . of a different and honest character".

Where, however, a person accused under the 1959 Act shows that he had not examined the article, and had no reasonable cause to suspect that it was obscene, he has a defence (*O.P.A.* 1959, *s.* 2).

11. 'Taken as a whole". The article must be considered "as a whole" (*O.P.A.* 1959, *s.* 1). Judges nowadays generally direct that the jury be supplied with copies of the article at the start of the trial, and often adjourn the hearing to enable them to read it in the jury room. Judges no longer permit the prosecution merely to read out, in isolation, the passages of which it complains.

In *The Philanderer* case, the judge told the jury to "consider the book as a whole, rather than pounce on single passages out of context".

The 1959 Act also provides (*see* 2) that, if the article comprises two or more distinct items, it shall be obscene if the effect of *one* of them, taken as a whole, would tend to deprave and corrupt. This provision was considered by Lord Widgery in *R.* v. *Anderson* (1974). An issue of *Oz* contained a number of articles, of some of which no complaint was made at all; but others were alleged to be obscene. Lord Widgery said that in the case of a novel, the publisher is entitled to have the work considered as a whole; but a magazine publisher, who has a far greater discretion on what to include or leave out, is to be judged under the item-by-item test—i.e., taking each item, but not the magazine, as a whole. If one item is obscene, it will taint the whole. Lord Widgery said: "Although it might seem unfair, it is unquestionably the law."

12. Obscenity not confined to sex. "Corruption may take . . . various forms. It may be to induce erotic desires of a heterosexual kind, or to promote homosexuality or other sexual perversions, or drug-taking or brutal violence" (Lord Justice Salmon in the *Last Exit* case).

Any belief that "obscenity" was confined to sex had been

dispelled in *John Calder Publications Ltd.* v. *Powell* (1965) when *Cain's Book*, describing the imaginary life of a junkie in New York, was held obscene. Mr. Justice Sachs observed the Oxford Dictionary definition of "obscene": "filthy, indecent, offensive to modesty or decency, expressing or suggesting lewd thoughts". He commented: "There is nothing there which limits it to a sexual sense."

In *D.P.P.* v. *A. and B.C. Chewing Gum Ltd.* (1968) it was not disputed that horrific "battle" pictures enclosed in packets of bubble gum could be obscene.

The *Children and Young Persons (Harmful Publications) Act* 1955 makes it an offence to publish in any book, magazine, or other work likely to fall into the hands of children or young persons—and consisting wholly or mainly of stories told in pictures, with or without written matter—stories portraying the commission of crimes, or acts of violence or cruelty, or "incidents of a repulsive or horrible nature", in such a way that the work as a whole would tend to corrupt a child or young persons.

Proceedings require the leave of the Attorney-General.

13. Forfeiture. The *O.P.A.* 1959, *s.* 3, provides:

"1. If a Justice of the Peace is satisfied from information on oath that there is reasonable ground for suspecting that on any premises in the petty sessions area for which he acts . . . being premises . . . specified in the information, obscene articles are, or are from time to time, kept for publication for gain, the justice may issue a warrant under his hand, empowering any constable to enter (if need be by force) and search the premises . . . within 14 days of the warrant, and to seize any articles found therein or thereon which the constable has reason to believe to be obscene articles, and to be kept for publication for gain.

"2. A warrant under the foregoing subsection shall, if any articles are seized under the warrant, also empower the seizure and removal of any documents found in the premises . . . which relate to a trade or business carried on at the premises . . .

"3. Any articles seized under subsection (1) of this section shall be brought before a Justice of the Peace acting for the same petty sessions area as the justice who issued the warrant, and the justice before whom the articles were brought may thereupon issue a summons to the occupier of the premises . . . to appear on a day specified in the summons before a magistrates court for that petty sessions area to show cause why the articles or any of them should not be forfeited; and if the court is satisfied as respects any of the articles that, at the time when they were seized, they were obscene articles kept for publication for gain, the court shall order those articles to be forfeited.

"4. In addition to the person summoned, any other person, being the owner, author or maker of the articles brought before the court, or any other person through whose hands they had passed before being seized, shall be entitled to appear before the court on the day specified to show cause why they should not be forfeited."

NOTE: any person who appeared, *or was entitled to appear*, on a summons for forfeiture, is also entitled to appeal to the Crown Court against a forfeiture order (*s.* 3(5) *O.P.A.* 1959). He has 21 days in which to give notice of appeal (*Crown Court Rules* 1971, *r.* 7).

Sub-section (7) goes on: "For the purposes of this section, the question whether an article is obscene shall be determined on the assumption that copies of it would be published in any manner likely having regard to the circumstances in which it was found, but in no other manner." In *Morgan* v. *Bowker* (1964) it was held that the court must not exclude evidence tendered by the defence about the circumstances in which the articles were found, the type of business carried on there, etc.

"PUBLIC GOOD"

14. Defence of "public good". Section 4(1), *O.P.A.* 1959, provides:

"A person shall not be convicted of an offence under *s.* 2 of this Act, [publishing an obscene article] and an order for forfeiture shall not be made, if it is proved that the publication of the article in question was justified as being for the public good on the ground that it is in the interest of science, literature, art or learning, or of other objects of general concern."

15. Expert witnesses. In establishing a defence of "public good", expert witnesses may be called. Section 4(2), *O.P.A.* 1959 provides:

"It is hereby declared that the opinion of experts as to the literary, artistic, scientific or other merits of an article may be admitted in any proceedings under this Act, either to establish or to negative the said ground".

NOTE:

(*i*) The words "or to negative". The prosecution may call experts to say that the work is devoid of literary, etc., merit.

(*ii*) The defence of "public good" is available only in a prosecution under the *O.P.A.* 1959—not, e.g., in one for sending indecent matter through the post, or for conspiring to corrupt morals.

(*iii*) The court may reject the experts' views. In the *Cain's Book* case (*see* **12**) Lord Parker said this applied even if—as in that case—all the experts were unanimous in saying that the book had literary merit.

(*iv*) Evidence will not be admitted on whether the work is obscene. In *D.P.P.* v. *A. and B.C. Chewing Gum Ltd.* it was held that a psychiatrist's evidence was admissible as to the likely effect of "battle" pictures on children's minds. But that decision should be considered highly exceptional, said Lord Widgery in the *Oz* case (*see* **11**). He added: "In the ordinary run-of-the-mill case in the future, the issue of obscene or no must be tried by the jury without the assistance of experts' evidence. Some might think that unnecessarily restrictive, but they must campaign for a change in the law."

(*v*) In *D.P.P.* v. *Staniforth* (1976) the House of Lords held that the "other merits" referred to in *s.* 4(2) do not include everything which may benefit the public, so that it is no defence that pornography may have a therapeutic value in relieving the tensions of sexual deviants. In *R.* v. *Hanau* (1976)—the *Inside Linda Lovelace* case—a doctor gave evidence that the book provided "masturbatory material", but such evidence can no longer be admitted in the light of *Staniforth*.

16. Jury's function where "public good" is pleaded.
Lord Justice Salmon said in the *Last Exit* case:

". . . the jury must consider, on the one hand, the number of readers they believe would tend to be corrupted and depraved by the book, the strength of the tendency to corrupt and deprave, and the nature of the corruption and depravity. On the other hand they should assess the strength of the literary, sociological or ethical merit which they consider the book to possess. They should then weigh up all these factors and decide whether, on balance, the publication is proved to be justified as being for the public good."

OTHER OBSCENITY OFFENCES

17. Conspiracy. It is unlawful at common law to conspire to corrupt public morals or outrage public decency.

In *Shaw* v. *D.P.P.* (1962) the House of Lords held that the courts had a residual power to enforce "the supreme and fundamental purpose of the law"—the conservation of not only the safety and order, but also the moral welfare, of the state. Shaw had published a *Ladies' Directory*—a booklet listing the addresses and services of prostitutes. He was convicted of conspiring (i.e. with the prostitutes) to corrupt public morals.

In *Knuller* v. *D.P.P.* (1973) the magazine *IT* carried a column headed "males", consisting of advertisements for homosexual partners. The proprietors were convicted of conspiring to corrupt public morals.

They pointed out in vain that the homosexual advertisements in *IT* occupied only one column (in the *Ladies Directory* the advertisements formed almost the whole publication) and homosexual acts between consenting adults in private were, by 1973, no longer unlawful.

Lord Diplock, dissenting, lent judicial weight to many lawyers' dislike of conspiracy charges in obscenity cases:

"Most conduct which is offensive to public morals or public decency is prohibited by statute, or falls within the ambit of some specific misdemeanour at common law which has long been recognised in decided cases. Having regard to the content of some of the advertisements which were the subject matter of the charges in the instant case, and to the provision of facilities for forwarding to the advertisers answers to such advertisements, the defendants might well have been guilty of an offence under the *Obscene Publications Acts* 1959 and 1964, or of the common law misdemeanour of inciting or procuring the commission of the statutory offence of doing acts of gross indecency with male persons under 21."

In 1976, the Law Commission suggested, but not as a concluded view, the abolition of these conspiracy offences, and suggested that there could be legislation to deal with any resulting lacunae in the law.

18. Sending indecent matter through the post. The *Post Office Act* 1953, *s.* 11(1), provides:

"A person shall not send or attempt to send or procure to be sent a postal packet which . . . (b) encloses any indecent or obscene print, painting, photograph, lithograph, engraving, cinematographic film, book, card or written communication, or any indecent or obscene article, or (c) has on the packet, or on the cover thereof, any words, marks or designs which are grossly offensive or of an indecent or obscene character."

NOTE: the test under this Act is different from that under the Obscene Publications Acts. In the *Oz* case (*see* **11**) the editors' convictions under the *O.P.A.* 1959 were quashed, but those under the *Post Office Act* 1953 were upheld.

19. Importing indecent matter. The *Customs Consolidation Act* 1876, *s.* 42, prohibits importation of "indecent or obscene" works.

20. Other Acts against obscenity. Less commonly used statutes include: *Town Police Clauses Act* 1847; *Vagrancy Acts* 1824 and 1838; *Metropolitan Police Act* 1839. Some local authorities have bye-laws against various forms of obscenity.

21. Injunctions. In some cases, attempts have been made to obtain injunctions to stop publication of allegedly obscene matter.

In *Re X, a minor* (1974) a judge exercised his powers in the wardship of a girl of 14 to make an order restraining publication of the first chapter of a book describing the depravity of the girl's father, who had since died. It was felt that the chapter would cause grave injury to the girl's psychological and emotional health if she read it. The Court of Appeal quashed the order, holding that wardship jurisdiction ought not to prevail over the wider interests of freedom of speech and publication.

In *R.* v. *Independent Broadcasting Authority, ex parte McWhirter* (1973) Ross McWhirter tried unsuccessfully to get an injunction to stop the I.B.A. showing a film which he considered offensive.

PROGRESS TEST 12

1. Explain "obscenity" under the *Obscene Publications Act* 1959. **(3)**
2. "An allegedly obscene article must be considered as a whole." Explain in relation to (*a*) a book, and (*b*) a newspaper article. **(11)**
3. "Obscenity is not confined to sex." Explain. **(12)**

4. What is the "forfeiture" procedure under *s. 3, Obscene Publications Act* 1959? **(13)**

5. Explain the defence of "public good" and the functions in relation to it of (*a*) expert witnesses and (*b*) jurors. **(14–16)**

6. Explain the decisions in *Shaw* v. *D.P.P.* (1962) and *Knuller* v. *D.P.P.* (1973). **(17)**

7. "The test for obscenity under the *Obscene Publications Act* 1959 is different from that under the *Post Office Act* 1953"—explain. **(18)**

CHAPTER XIII

PRIVACY

JOURNALISTS AND THE PUBLIC INTEREST

1. Explanation. The law at present makes no express provisions for protecting the citizen's privacy—e.g. to protect a film actress from publicity about her latest love affair, or to shield persons from being photographed in public places against their will (except photographs in the precincts of a court, *see* X, **21**). Raymond Bellisario was unrepentant over his furtive pictures of members of the Royal Family, which he sold to continental magazines. "I have abided by the rules of this country; they allow me to take the photographs that I do."

2. Snooping. In 1972 a furore arose among some politicians over the methods used by the *News of the World* in obtaining evidence of the association of a government Minister with prostitutes. The newspaper arranged for them to be secretly photographed together in compromising circumstances, saying afterwards that it did not intend to publish the photographs, but merely to use them as evidence should the allegations be denied.

The *News of the World* claimed to have been acting in the public interest, and pointed out that without its investigation the Minister might have remained in office and have been "an obvious target for blackmail attempts by the country's enemies". It was censured by the Press Council—for allowing the material to be in unauthorised hands. The Press Council accepted that there might be situations where such methods were justified, but "the user of such methods, be he citizen or or press, employs them at the risk of his own reputation, and nothing but success is an acceptable excuse".

The Times used a tape recorder to obtain evidence of corruption against two police officers. Far from being censured, they were congratulated, both by the trial judge and by the Court of Appeal (*R.* v. *Robson and Harris* (1972)).

SOME OFFENCES

3. Offences involving snooping.

(a) *Conspiracy to trespass*. E.g. inquiry agents who trespassed in private premises in order to instal a "bug" to obtain evidence for divorce proceedings. (*R.* v. *Withers* (1971).)

(b) *Conspiracy to trick*. E.g. in *R.* v. *Quartermain* (1974), an inquiry agent obtained information from government, local authority and police departments by impersonating authorised persons.

(c) *Conspiracy to effect a public mischief*. However, in *D.P.P.* v. *Withers* (1974) inquiry agents who impersonated government and local authority departments in order to obtain information were held by the House of Lords not guilty of this offence.

(d) *Wireless Telegraphy Act* 1949. An inquiry agent who was said to have a "Watergate armoury" of bugging devices was convicted under this Act (*R.* v. *Quartermain* (1974), above). So, too, have been journalists who listened in to police, etc., wireless messages and made use of the information thereby obtained.

(e) *Rehabilitation of Offenders Act* 1974. Section (9)4 makes it an offence to obtain by fraud, dishonesty or bribery information about a person's "spent" convictions (*see* Chapter III).

(f) *Official Secrets Act* 1911, *s.* 2. To induce a public officer to part with information in breach of his duty would be an offence under this Act (*see* XVI, 7).

PRIVACY COMMITTEE'S VIEWS

4. Recommendations on snooping.

The Younger Committee on Privacy recommended that the use of electronic and optical devices for surveillance should be made a criminal offence, and "the law in this as in other matters should apply to those working for the press as it does to all other persons". (No member of the public had complained of the press using such devices.)

The Law Commission (Working Paper 54) invited views on a possible new offence of "entering and remaining on property" for the purpose of surveillance.

5. Harassment. The Younger Committee said the complaints which it had received about journalists' intrusion related to harassment. Instances given to the Committee were few, "but the Press Council's proceedings show that reporters do at times pursue their inquiries beyond the point that people consider reasonable".

The instances were: pestering occupants of a private house to obtain material for an article on witchcraft; calling late at night on a couple in their remote holiday house, at the end of a day when police had been seeking a man who had attacked their daughter; and two cases involving the handing over of children by their foster parents to their natural parents, under compulsion of court orders. The Committee's decision on intrusion into privacy was that:

(a) Invasion of privacy was justified only where the importance of the news exceeded the importance of the privacy.

(b) As to where that point lay, the Committee could devise no general rule to show at how late an hour a newspaperman would be justified in disturbing a private citizen, or for that matter a public figure, or how far he should pursue him to a holiday retreat to get information or comment, or how far the importance or urgency of the news should affect his decision.

(c) No flexible rule could be laid down that newspapers, when judging it necessary in the public interest to comment on the administration and discipline in a school, should not approach pupils or parents directly.

(d) Even where news "more obviously concerns matters in the private domain, or relates to single individuals of no public status, there is room for two opinions on the newspapers' obligations".

6. Investigative journalism. The Younger Committee accepted that investigative journalism was in principle a legitimate function of the press "provided it is carried on within the same rules which bind the ordinary citizen and the working journalist alike".

(The Newspaper Publishers' Association had no success in persuading the Home Office that the *Rehabilitation of Offenders Act* 1974 should be amended so as not to inhibit investigative journalism.)

SOME PRESS COUNCIL ADJUDICATIONS

7. Scandal raking. In 1969 the *News of the World* published a young woman's memoirs, thereby exhuming the indiscretions of yet another public figure, six years earlier. The Press Council, censuring the newspaper, said it was a question of degree what events would justify dragging up the past of a man who had been involved in a scandal. The Council had previously condemned as "hounding" a case where the parents of a man who, six years earlier, had been convicted of murder, were named as they were about to emigrate. The Council thought the same protection should extend to a man who had been in a high rank in public life, unless the public interest justified reference to him.

In 1976, Mr. Harold Wilson, as he then was, called for agreement on a privacy code between the media and the government. The Press Council followed with a Declaration on Privacy: that information about private individuals' lives and concerns should not be published unless there is a legitimate public interest over-riding the right to privacy, and should not be pursued unless the editor considers at the time that such an interest—not mere prurient or morbid curiosity—might arise; and that the use of eavesdropping, or technological methods, or deception, or intrusion into private grief, could be justified only if the information sought ought in the public interest to be published, and could not be got by any other reasonably practicable method.

8. Other intrusions into privacy. In 1975 the Council adjudicated that newspapers should not publish photographs of funerals which were not "public occasions", or, without consent, pictures of the widow of a murdered man. In 1976, it condemned the identification in court reports of accused persons' relatives who were unconnected with the proceedings. In another 1976 adjudication, it said private letters about private matters should generally not be published without their writers' consents, at least during their lifetimes; but publication without consent might be justified where the subject matter was "in truth of public interest", e.g. if it concerned "bodies which are or have been engaged in political or industrial activities".

9. Assault by camera. In 1975 proceedings were begun in Scotland against some press photographers who were said to have photographed persons against their will, it being alleged that they had "assaulted" them by camera. The proceedings were discontinued. It is inconceivable that such a summons could succeed in English law.

PROGRESS TEST 13

1. Reconcile the censure of the *News of the World* and the congratulation of reporters of *The Times* over the use of surreptitious surveillance devices. **(2)**

2. How did the *News of the World* seek to justify its action in surreptitiously photographing a Government minister with a prostitute ? **(2)**

3. Describe some of the offences which may arise from "snooping". **(3)**

4. In what circumstances did the Younger Committee consider the invasion of privacy justified ? **(5)**

5. What was the Younger Committee's view of investigative journalism ? **(6)**

CHAPTER XIV

CONFIDENTIAL INFORMATION

1. Explanation. A court will grant an injunction to prevent the wrongful disclosure of information which has been obtained in circumstances of confidentiality. The *Supreme Court of Judicature (Consolidation) Act* 1925, *s.* 45(1), enables the High Court to grant an injunction "where it appears to the court to be just or convenient to do so". Most High Court judges ensure, however, that an injunction is not used as a form of censorship merely to prevent publication of something which the plaintiff does not like (cf. the words of Mr. Justice O'Connor in VI, **24**).

2. Information acquired in course of employment. "When a person obtains information in the course of a confidential employment, the law does not permit him to make any improper use of the information so obtained"—Mr. Justice North in *Pollard* v. *Photographic Co.* (1889).

The Royal Family has provided numerous instances. Example:

> In 1960, a former footman to Princess Margaret proposed to publish his "memoirs" in a Paris newspaper. The Princess was granted an injunction restraining him from disclosing "any incident or conversation which may be within his knowledge by reason of his having been in the plaintiff's [the Princess's] service", or "any information regarding the plaintiff or any member of the Royal Family or regarding any matter which might concern them which might be communicated to the press".

An injunction will also be granted to stop an ex-employee disclosing trade secrets—e.g. secret processes—of his former employer (*Printers and Finishers Ltd.* v. *Holloway* (1964)).

In *Seager* v. *Copydex* (1969) the Court of Appeal said there was a duty, *irrespective of any contract*, not to take unfair advantage of information which had been received in confidence.

In *Distillers Co. (Biochemicals) Ltd.* v. *Times Newspapers Ltd.* (1974) *The Sunday Times* was restrained from making use of

information about the drug Thalidomide which had been
prepared in connection with pending litigation.

3. No injunction if no confidentiality. In 1970 a judge
refused an injunction to stop B.B.C. Television screening a
programme about a London hotel in which some of the
employees complained about their working conditions. No
breach of confidence in the master-and-servant relationship
was involved.

4. No injunction if against public policy. An injunction
will not be granted if disclosure is in the public interest.

In *Initial Services Ltd.* v. *Putterill* (1968) a laundry company's
former sales manager passed to the *Daily Mail* information on
the basis of which the newspaper carried stories alleging a
liaison between launderers to keep up prices. In proceedings
against Mr. Putterill and the newspaper, the company alleged
infringement of an implied term in Mr. Putterill's contract of
service that he would not disclose confidential information. The
court held on an interlocutory appeal that such a duty did not
extend to information which ought, in the public interest, to be
disclosed to a person having a proper interest to receive it. And,
said Lord Denning:

   "... there may be cases where the misdeed is of such a
   character that the public interest may demand, or at least
   excuse, publication on a much broader field, even to the press".

In 1972 the Church of Scientology sought an injunction to
restrain publication of *The Mind Benders*, by Cyril Vosper, a
former member of the cult. They alleged misuse of confidential
information. An injunction was refused. Lord Denning said
Mr. Vosper had put forward a defence of public interest, and
"if what he says is true it is only right that the dangers of the
cult should be exposed".

Just as the court would not restrain a defendant in a libel
action if he said he was going to justify, so it should not restrain
him in an action for alleged breach of confidence if he said he
had a defence of public interest. (*Hubbard* v. *Vosper* (1972).)

5. The extent of public interest. The Law Commission, in
its Working Paper 58 on Confidential Information, suggested:

"It is perhaps arguable that it would be in the public interest to disclose that a public company had taken, or was about to take, a decisive step—such as entering into a contract to remove part of its works elsewhere—which would entail the dismissal of 10,000 men with no other prospects of local employment; but that the public interest could not possibly justify the disclosure of a purely preliminary discussion of a board of directors when the possibility of taking drastic action of this kind to save the company was merely canvassed."

6. Only the injured party may seek injunction. In *Fraser* v. *Evans* (1969) *The Sunday Times* obtained a copy of a written report made by a public relations consultant to the Greek government. The consultant sought unsuccessfully to restrain publication. Lord Denning said the consultant's duty of confidence was owed to the Greek government, which alone could seek an injunction.

7. "Wearing two hats." In an adjudication in 1974, the Press Council said a reporter who attends a meeting in a private capacity—e.g. as a committee member—should not make journalistic use of information thereby acquired.

8. Cabinet secrets: the Crossman Diaries case. In 1975 the Attorney-General sought orders preventing *The Sunday Times* and book publishers from publishing some of the diaries of the late Richard Crossman, relating to his time as a Cabinet minister.

Lord Widgery said Cabinet confidence was imposed to enable the efficient conduct of the Queen's business. The confidence was owed to the Queen, and could not be released by Cabinet ministers themselves.

In this case, however, the first volume of the diaries dealt with events of ten years and three general elections earlier, and he could not believe that publication would inhibit free discussion in the present-day Cabinet. But he warned that "different considerations" might apply to the remainder of the Crossman Diaries, dealing with more recent events.

"The degree of protection afforded to Cabinet papers and discussions cannot be determined by a single rule of thumb. Some secrets require a high standard of protection for a short time. Others may require protection until a new political generation has taken over."

If a court could prohibit the disclosure of domestic secrets (*see* **9**) he could not see why it should be powerless to stop publication of national secrets.

The Crown decided not to appeal, because the judgment had recognised the principle that Cabinet secrets could be protected by injunction (*Attorney-General* v. *Jonathan Cape Ltd.* (1975)).

In 1975 a committee of Privy Councillors recommended a voluntary code which should, *inter alia*, protect Cabinet secrets for up to 15 years.

9. Family and matrimonial secrets. The courts will restrain the disclosure of information which has been obtained by the defendant by reason of his membership of a family or a marriage.

> After the dissolution of the marriage of the Duke and Duchess of Argyll, the Duke began to write a series of articles about the Duchess's private life, two of which were published in *The People*. The Duchess sought an injunction against the Duke, and against the newspaper's editor and publishers, to stop further publication of "secrets relating to her private life". HELD: the material intended for publication constituted a breach of marital confidence, and would also be a breach of the *Judicial Proceedings* (*Regulation of Reports*) *Act* 1926. "The court, in the exercise of its equitable jurisdiction, will restrain a breach of confidence independently of any right at law." (*Duchess of Argyll* v. *Duke of Argyll* (1967)).

The Court of Appeal has refused to prevent publication of a chapter of a book which described a father's depravity. Lord Denning said an injunction would impinge too much on the freedom of the press (*In Re X, a minor* (1974)—*see* XII, **21**).

10. Spent convictions. *See* X, **20** for the offence under *s.* 9, *Rehabilitation of Offenders Act* 1974, of disclosing a "spent" conviction.

11. Search of premises. In *Piller* v. *Manufacturing Processes* (1975) the Court of Appeal decided that it had power to order the search of premises where confidential papers were alleged to be wrongfully kept, but would do so only in exceptional circumstances.

12. Proposed new tort. The Law Commission, in Working Paper 58, put forward the (provisional, but not conclusive) suggestion that a duty of confidence should be owed by a person who knows, or ought to know, that information has reached him directly or indirectly through another person who received it in confidence; and that a person to whom such a duty of confidence is owed should have a right to recover damages for wrongful disclosure if it caused him distress and would be likely to cause distress to a reasonable person.

PROGRESS TEST 14

1. In what circumstances will the courts restrain publication of confidential information ? **(1, 2, 8, 9)**

2. In what circumstances will they not do so ? **(3, 4, 6)**

3. How far did the Law Commission consider that public interest in disclosure of confidential information extended ? **(5)**

4. To what protection, if any, did Lord Widgery, in *Attorney-General* v. *Jonathan Cape Ltd.* (1975) consider Cabinet secrets to be entitled ? **(8)**

5. Explain the reasons for the decision in the *Argyll* marriage secrets case. **(9)**

CHAPTER XV

COPYRIGHT

PROTECTION AGAINST PIRACY

1. Explanation. The law of copyright exists to protect against misuse of other people's original literary, dramatic, artistic or musical works.

2. Meaning of copyright. Copyright means the exclusive right to do, and authorise others to do, certain acts in relation to the copyright works (e.g. reproduce them—*see* **19**, below) in the United Kingdom (*Copyright Act* 1956, *s.* 1(1)). The definition also extends to works emanating from other countries specified in Orders made under the Act (*see* **35**).

Infringement of copyright should be distinguished from breach of confidence. "A flagrant breach of confidence may not be the same thing as a flagrant breach of copyright"—Mr. Justice Ungoed-Thomas in *Beloff* v. *Pressdram Ltd.* (1973).

COPYRIGHT IN LITERARY WORKS

3. Copyright in unpublished literary works. Copyright subsists in every original literary work which is unpublished, and of which the author was a "qualified person" at the time when the work was made, or, if the making of the work extended over a period, for a substantial part of that period (*C.A.* 1956, *s.* 2(1)). A "qualified person" is a British subject, or British protected person, or a citizen of the Irish Republic, or, if not coming within any of those categories, is domiciled or resident in the United Kingdom or in any other country to which the relevant provision of the *C.A.* 1956 extends. The definition also includes a body corporate (e.g. a company).

4. Copyright in published literary works. Where an original work has been published, copyright shall subsist or continue to subsist in it if, but only if, its first publication took place in the U.K. or another specified country; *or* the author was a qualified person at the time of first publication; *or* the author had died before that time, but was a qualified person immediately before his death (*C.A.* 1956, *s.* 2(2)).

5. Duration of copyright in literary works. Copyright in a literary work shall continue for fifty years from the end of the calendar year in which the author died (*C.A.* 1956, *s.* 2(3)). But if the work was not published or broadcast before that date, the fifty-year period shall run from the end of the calendar year in which the earliest publishing or broadcasting occurred.

The reference to "publishing" and "broadcasting" apply equally if what is published or broadcast is an adaptation of the work in question.

6. Copyright in anonymous works. Where the first publication of a literary work is anonymous or pseudonymous, any copyright in it shall run for fifty years from the end of the calendar year in which the work was first published. This does not apply if, at any time during those fifty years, a person without previous knowledge of the facts could, by reasonable inquiry, ascertain the author's identity (*C.A.* 1956, 2nd Sch.).

7. Copyright in works by joint authors. Here the fifty-year period runs from the end of the calendar year in which the last of the joint authors dies. If the identity of one of the joint authors is not disclosed, the period runs from the end of the calendar year in which the last "disclosed" author dies. But a joint author is deemed to be "disclosed" if the work was published under his real name, or if his identity could have been ascertained by reasonable inquiry (*C.A.* 1956, 3rd Sch.).

8. Meaning of "literary work". A judge once said it was difficult to define "literary work", but suggested: "Work which is expressed in print or writing, irrespective of the question whether the quality or style is high" (*University of London Press* v. *University Tutorial Press* (1916)).

The *C.A.* 1956, *s.* 48, provides that "literary work" includes any written table or compilation—e.g. Stock Exchange prices, or sports results.

A news agency acquired stock exchange prices at intervals during the day, and communicated them to its subscribers through its wire service. A non-subscriber obtained the service from a subscriber, and published the prices. The news agency was granted an injunction to restrain this misuse (*Exchange Telegraph Co.* v. *Gregory* (1896)).

The same news agency also supplied a horse race results service to subscribers. A rival news agency picked up this service and disseminated it to its own subscribers. An injunction was granted (*Exchange Telegraph Co.* v. *Central News* (1897)).

NOTE: In each of those cases, the agreement whereby subscribers received the Extel service provided that it should not be communicated to non-subscribers, but there would plainly have been a breach of copyright even without this provision.

9. Skill and labour essential. To qualify for copyright, a literary work need have no literary merit (*see*, for example, the *Exchange Telegraph* cases, **8**). Thus, copyright has been held to subsist in a football pool coupon (*Ladbrokes* (*Football*) *Ltd.* v. *William Hill* (*Football*) *Ltd.* (1964)). But the work must involve some skill or labour. Thus no copyright exists in part of a sheet for recording cricket scores (*Page* v. *Wisden* (1869))—though a copyright would exist in the scores after they had been recorded.

10. Ideas are not "literary work". Ideas, however novel, do not qualify for copyright unless they are put on to paper.

Interviews with Steven Donoghue, the jockey, appeared in the *News of the World*. Extracts were reproduced in *Guide and Ideas*. Donoghue sued for breach of copyright. HELD: the copyright was not his (*Donoghue* v. *Allied Newspapers Ltd.* (1938)).

11. Meaning of "original". "Novelty and inventiveness are not the tests of originality . . . . The test is whether the design is original in the sense that it is the original expression of the thought of its creator" (Mr. Justice Judson in *Kilvington Brothers* v. *Goldberg* (1957)).

In *Walter* v. *Lane* (1900) *The Times* published verbatim reports of speeches by Lord Rosebery. These were reproduced almost exactly by the defendant. HELD: *The Times* had acquired a copyright in its reports of the speeches.

NOTE: This case was decided under the *Copyright Act* 1842, which contained no requirement that the work should be "original". But it is submitted that in such circumstances the "originality" is supplied by reducing the speech to writing. It was conceded that the newspaper would have had no copyright if Lord Rosebery had read his speeches from manuscripts.

12. No copyright in news. No copyright subsists in news, but it may subsist in its literary presentation.

A newspaper infringed copyright by copying from *The Times* long extracts from an article by Rudyard Kipling. Mr. Justice North said: "It is said that there is no copyright in news; but there is, or may be, copyright in the particular forms of language or modes of expression by which the information is conveyed, and not the less so because the information may be with respect to the current events of the day." (*Walter* v. *Steinkopf* (1892)).

13. No copyright in a title. Titles of books or other publications will not generally enjoy copyright.

World, a sixpenny newspaper, published a novel, "Splendid Misery", unaware that another novel of that name had been published some four years earlier in *Every Week*, a penny newspaper. HELD: no infringement. There was no possibility of the public being misled (*Dicks* v. *Yates* (1881)).

An injunction may be granted where such a possibility arises (though in *Borthwick* v. *The Evening Post* (1888) it was held that actual damage must also be shown). In *D.C. Thomson & Co. Ltd.* v. *Kent Messenger Ltd.* (1974) the publishers of the *Sunday Post* in Scotland failed to get an injunction to stop the launching of the *South East Sunday Post* in Kent. In *Baylis & Co.* (*Maidenhead Advertiser*) *Ltd.* v. *Darlenko Ltd.* (1974) the publishers of the *Maidenhead Advertiser* failed to stop the use of the name *The New Advertiser* for a free sheet circulating in their area. In each case it was held there was insufficient likelihood of substantial confusion.

14. No copyright in obscene, etc., works. On grounds of public policy the courts will not extend the protection of copyright to works which are obscene or libellous. (*Ex turpe causa non oritur actio*: "no action arises from a base cause".)

Infringement was alleged in the reproduction of a number of articles and pictures entitled *La Panorama*. HELD: there was an infringement in respect of most of the work, but not in respect of two of the pictures because they were indecent (*Baschet* v. *London Illustrated Standard Co.* (1900)).

A similar view once extended to blasphemous works, but modern attitudes may have changed this judicial approach. In *Chaplin* v. *Frewin Publishers Ltd.* (1966) some passages in a book by Charles Chaplin's son were thought by two Court of Appeal judges to be blasphemous, but it was held nevertheless that the author had a binding contract with the publishers.

The same view probably applies to attacks on the monarchy, which in earlier times would have been seditious, if not treasonable.

15. Letters to the editor. A letter, or other unsolicited manuscript sent gratuitously to the editor of a newspaper for possible publication, becomes the property of the newspaper. Where there is an intention to give, plus delivery, there is a gift of a document just as of any other species of personal property:

> Dylan Thomas lost the manuscript of *Under Milk Wood*. He told a B.B.C. producer that he could have the manuscript if he could find it, and suggested some public houses where he might look. The producer found it in one of them. After Dylan Thomas's death, his widow sought to recover the manuscript. HELD: he made a gift of it (*Thomas* v. *Times Book Co. Ltd.* (1966)).

Although the document itself becomes the property of the donee, the copyright does not (an assignment of it would in any event need to be expressly in writing—*see* 33). The writer of a letter to the editor impliedly grants a licence to publish it on one occasion, but no more.

16. Submitted copy. Where a manuscript is submitted for possible publication for payment, if there is in law an "offer" of the manuscript, it may be inferred that the publisher can accept the offer by publishing the manuscript and impliedly agreeing to make reasonable payment for it. If, on the other hand, the submission of the manuscript is a mere "invitation to treat", the author is inviting the publisher to make an offer which he (the author) may accept or reject.

A journalist who telephones copy to a newspaper which does not employ him does not thereby divest himself of the copyright (this would need to be done in writing—*see* 33). Even if he submitted the copy in writing, he would not divest himself of the copyright unless he expressly assigned it in writing. In the absence of agreement to the contrary, he impliedly licenses the newspaper to make use of his copy in consideration of an implied promise to make reasonable payment, while he reserves the right to make whatever other use of it he chooses.

17. Criticisms or reviews. No fair dealing with a literary work shall constitute an infringement of copyright if it is for the purpose of criticism or review, whether of that work or of another work, and is accompanied by a sufficient acknowledgement. Nor will such fair dealing be an infringement if it is for the purpose of reporting current events in a newspaper, magazine or similar periodical, or by means of broadcasting or film (*C.A.* 1956, *s.* 6).

"Fair dealing" means the quoting of limited extracts from copyright works for the above purposes, but for no ulterior purpose. Example:

> A publisher reproduced, without permission, caricatures from past copies of *Punch*. The Court of Exchequer accepted that some reproduction would, in the right circumstances, be permissible. Baron Bramwell said: "If the defendant had said: 'I propose to illustrate my history by extracts from the satirists of the day', and had then gone on to quote to a reasonable extent the opinions, and even the very words, of the satirical writers, no one would call that piracy." But, said the Baron, the defendant had exceeded the permissible bounds of quotation because his purpose was the same as that for which the caricatures were originally produced—to excite readers' amusement.

> NOTE: the Act provides that the quotation may be from a different work from that which is being reviewed—e.g. for purposes of comparison.

An injunction will not be granted in interlocutory proceedings for breach of copyright if the defendant intends to plead fair dealing (*Hubbard* v. *Vosper* (1972)).

The *C.A.* 1956, *s.* 6, also provides that copyright in a literary work is not infringed by reproducing it for purposes of a judicial proceeding, or a report of a judicial proceeding.

18. No copyright in a nom de plume. There is generally no copyright in a nom de plume. But where confusion might arise, an injunction will be granted. Example:

> A cartoonist known professionally as "Kem" complained that a newspaper published cartoons by another cartoonist who

signed himself "Kim", the signatures looking somewhat similar.
HELD: although the signatures were not identical, there was a
clear possibility of confusion, and an injunction would be granted
(*Marengo* v. *Daily Sketch* (1948)).

Where a nom de plume has become identified with a particular
writer, and that writer ceases to write for the journal in which
his pseudonymous work has appeared, the court will restrain
the continued use of the nom de plume by the journal. Example:

Gertrude Landa wrote a children's column in a Jewish newspaper under the name "Aunt Naomi". After she had left the
newspaper, it issued membership cards of its Young Israel
League bearing the words "conducted by Aunt Naomi". HELD:
Miss Landa had become identified with "Aunt Naomi", and the
continued use by the newspaper of that nom de plume was
calculated to lead to the belief that the Young Israel League
was still being conducted by her (*Landa* v. *Greenberg* (1908)).

This rule applies even if the nom de plume was suggested by
the editor.

Miss Forbes was engaged by a Sunday newspaper to write a
women's column under the pseudonym "Marie Delane". In time,
considerable good will attached to her column. HELD: she was
entitled to take the name with her as part of her stock in trade
(*Forbes* v. *Kemsley Newspapers Ltd.* (1951)).

**19. Restricted acts in relation to copyright literary
works.** The *C.A.* 1956, *s.* 2(5), provides that the acts restricted
by copyright in a literary work are: reproducing it in any
material form, publishing it, causing it to be transmitted to
subscribers in a diffusion service, and making any adaptation
of it (this would include translation into another language, or
into another form: e.g. a dramatic work into a novel, or vice
versa, or into a strip-cartoon).

Section 5 provides that copyright is infringed by any person
who, in the United Kingdom or in any of the specified foreign
countries, "sells, lets for hire, or by way of trade offers or
exposes for sale or hire any article, or by way of trade exhibits
any article in public, if it is to his knowledge that the making
of the article constituted an infringement of that copyright or
[in the case of an imported article] would have constituted an
infringement of that copyright if the article had been made in
the place into which it was imported".

20. Use of another's name in by-line. The *C.A.* 1956, *s.* 43, makes it actionable as a breach of statutory duty to affix another's name in or on a work of which he was not the author, in such a way as to imply that he was the author.

In an action over a newspaper article "When love turns sour, by Dorothy Squires" the singer recovered damages under *s.* 43 notwithstanding the addition of the words, in smaller print, "talking to Weston Taylor" (*Moore* v. *News of the World Ltd.* (1972)).

COPYRIGHT IN ARTISTIC WORKS

21. Definition of "artistic work". Artistic works include "paintings, sculptures, drawings, engravings and photographs" "irrespective of artistic quality" (*C.A.* 1956, *s.* 3(1)). The definition also extends to "other works of artistic craftsmanship" (*C.A.* 1956, *s.* 3(1) (c)).

By *s.* 48(1), "drawing" includes any diagram, map, chart or plan; "engraving" includes any etching, lithograph, woodcut, print or similar work, not being a photograph; and "photograph" means any product of photography or any process akin to photography, other than part of a cinematograph film.

William Strange, a publisher, obtained some drawings and etchings which Queen Victoria and Prince Albert had made of their children. He proposed to exhibit copies of them, and publish a catalogue. Prince Albert was granted an injunction to stop him (*Prince Albert* v. *Strange* (1849)).

22. Published and unpublished artistic work. The provisions relating to copyright in published and unpublished literary works apply, *mutatis mutandis*, to published and unpublished artistic works.

23. Duration of copyright in artistic works. Copyright runs for fifty years from the end of the calendar year in which the author died. Copyright in a photograph runs for fifty years from the end of the calendar year in which the photograph is first published (*C.A.* 1956, *s.* 3(4) (*b*)).

24. Restricted acts in relation to copyright artistic works. These are: reproducing the work in any material form; publishing it; and including it in a television broadcast.

25. No copyright in ideas. It is the maker of the artistic work, and not the person—if different—whose idea it was who owns the copyright. Example:

> A spiritualist medium drew a portrait of a deceased young man, claiming that the image had come to him from the spirit world. HELD: whether or not this claim was right, it was the medium who, by putting the image on to paper, was entitled to copyright in it—and not the young man's father, for whom he drew it, or still less, the spirit (*Leah* v. *Two Worlds Publishing Co. Ltd.* (1951)).

But *see* **30** for the position where a portrait, etc., is "commissioned".

26. Review, etc., of artistic works. The *C.A.* 1956, *s.* 9(2), provides: "No fair dealing with an artistic work shall constitute an infringement of copyright if it is for the purposes of criticism or review, whether of that work or of another work, and is accompanied by a sufficient acknowledgement".

Nor is there any infringement if the reproduction is for the purpose of a judicial proceeding or a report of such proceeding (*s.* 9(7)).

The inclusion of an artistic work in a television broadcast or in a film does not infringe copyright if the inclusion is only incidental or by way of background.

27. Use of another's name. The provisions of *s.* 43 (*see* **20**) apply equally to artistic works.

COPYRIGHT IN WORK OF EMPLOYEES

28. Newspaper, etc., employees. The *C.A.* 1956, *s.* 4(2), provides:

> "Where a literary, dramatic or artistic work is made by the author in the course of his employment by the proprietor of a newspaper, magazine or similar periodical under a contract of service or apprenticeship, and is so made for the purpose of publication in a newspaper, magazine or similar periodical, the said proprietor shall be entitled to the copyright in the work in so far as the copyright relates to the publication of the work in any newspaper, magazine or similar periodical or to reproduction of the work for the purpose of its being so published; but in all

other respects the author shall be entitled to any copyright subsisting in the work".

Nora Beloff, political columnist of *The Observer*, alleged infringement of copyright by the magazine *Private Eye* in reproducing extracts from her work. HELD: the copyright belonged to the newspaper, and not to Miss Beloff, because she was an employee and not an independent contractor (*Beloff* v. *Pressdram Ltd.* (1973)).

In deciding whether a person is an employee or an independent contractor, a court will have regard to, e.g., the degree of control which the employer has over the method by which the person carries out his work, the way in which the person is remunerated, the bases on which he pays income tax and national insurance contributions, and whether he is generally an integral part of the business, or merely ancillary to it.

29. Work of employees generally. The *C.A.* 1956, *s.* 4(4) provides that where, in the case of non-newspaper employees, a work is made by an author in the course of his employment, the copyright shall vest in the employer.

An accountant, who was an expert in business management, purported to assign to publishers the copyright in a series of his lectures, based on his experience acquired during his employment by the plaintiffs. HELD: the author's knowledge, skill and know-how were his own property, notwithstanding that they were acquired during his employment, and the major part of his manuscript was thus not made during "the course of his employment". Part of it, however, had been prepared for the purposes of a particular assignment for the employer, and copyright in this part vested in the employer. This part was severable from the rest of the manuscript. (*Stevenson, Jordan & Harrison Ltd.* v. *Macdonald and Evans* (1952)).

30. Commissioned portraits, etc. The *C.A.* 1956, *s.* 4(3), provides: ". . . where a person commissions the taking of a photograph, or the painting or drawing of a portrait . . . and pays or agrees to pay for it in money or money's worth, and the work is made in pursuance of that commission, the person who so commissioned the work shall be entitled to any copyright subsisting therein. . ." Example:

The defendant was commissioned to take photographs of the plaintiff's wedding. Two years later the plaintiff's father-in-law, who appeared in the photographs, was murdered, and the defendant sold prints of the photographs to national newspapers. HELD: as the photographs were commissioned by the plaintiff, the copyright vested in him and not in the photographer (*Williams* v. *Settle* (1960)).

NOTE: such an infringement could, if the plaintiff took action in time, be restrained by injunction: *Pollard* v. *Photographic Co.* (1889)).

31. Work of employed photographer. Subject to the provisions in **2–30**, the author of a photograph is entitled to the copyright. "Author" of a photograph is defined in *s.* 48(1) as "the person who, at the time a photograph is taken, is the owner of the material on which it is taken." Thus, where a staff photographer uses his employer's photographic materials, the copyright must vest in his employer.

REMEDIES, ASSIGNMENT, ETC.

32. Remedies for infringement of copyright. The plaintiff in an action for breach of copyright may claim damages, an injunction, an order for the taking of accounts, and such other relief as is available for the infringement of proprietary rights (*C.A.* 1956, *s.* 17(1)).

(*a*) *Innocent infringement:* where, at the time of the infringement, the defendant was not aware, and had no reasonable grounds for suspecting, that copyright subsisted in the work, the plaintiff is not entitled to damages for the infringement, but shall be entitled to an account of profits in respect of the infringement, whether any other relief is granted or not (*C.A.* 1956, *s.* 17(2)).

(*b*) *Flagrant infringement:* where the court is satisfied, having regard to the flagrancy of the infringement, and any benefit shown to have accrued to the defendant by it, that effective relief would not otherwise by available to the plaintiff, it shall have power to award such additional damages as it may consider appropriate (*s.* 17(3)). In extreme cases, the court may order a search of premises for infringing material (*Piller* v. *Manufacturing Processes* (1975)).

(*c*) *Presumptions:* copyright is presumed to subsist in a work, and to belong to the plaintiff, unless the defendant puts these matters in issue (*s.* 20(1)). The person whose name appears on the work shall, unless the contrary is proved, be presumed to be the author, and not to have made the work in the course of any contract of employment (*s.* 20(2)).

33. Assignment of copyright. No assignment of copyright, whether total or partial, shall have effect unless in writing signed by or on behalf of the assignor (*s.* 36(3)).

An agreement may be made whereby copyright in future material vests in the assignee as soon as the agreement is made (e.g. an author may assign to publishers the copyright in a book he is about to write) (*s.* 37).

34. Effect of assignment. The assignee alone has the right to reproduce the copyright material. Example:

> Dr. Granville, an expert on watering places, assigned to publishers the manuscript on his visits to English spas. The publishers, on discovering that another publisher was producing a "Handbook of the hot springs of Bath" by Dr. Granville, obtained an injunction to stop them (*Colburn* v. *Simms* (1843)).

In the case of an artistic work, there is no infringement if the author produces a subsequent work by using a sketch, plan, mould, etc., used for the copyright work, if in making the subsequent work he does not repeat or imitate the main design of the copyright work (*s.* 9(9)).

An assignment may be avoided if it is inequitable. In *Schroeder Music Publishing Co. Ltd.* v. *Macaulay* (1974) the copyright in a song writer's works was assigned to a publisher under an agreement which did not oblige the publisher to make efforts to publish the songs. The agreement was avoided.

35. Crown Copyright. The Crown has a copyright in the Authorised Version of The Bible and the Book of Common Prayer. The *C.A.* 1956, *s.* 39, further provides that every literary or artistic work made by, or under the direction or control of, Her Majesty or a government department, shall be the subject of copyright, even if copyright would not otherwise subsist in the work.

If the work is unpublished, the copyright shall continue for so long as it so remains. If it is published, copyright shall subsist or continue for fifty years from the end of the calendar year in which the work is published.

36. International copyright. A number of treaties have been made between Great Britain and certain other countries, the effect of which has been to secure protection for copyright material beyond national frontiers. The first was the Berne Convention of 1885, followed by the *International Copyright Act* 1886—which was passed to enable Orders in Council to give effect to international conventions. The Berne Convention has been revised at a number of subsequent conventions, the last in Stockholm in 1967.

This Convention provides that authors shall enjoy, in Convention countries, the same protection for their works that the works enjoy in their country of origin—as well as the rights specially granted by the Convention. Nationals of a Convention country receive protection in every Convention country for both published and unpublished works, whether or not publication has taken place in a Convention country. The term of protection must not exceed, in other countries, the duration of the protection granted in the country of origin. The most common period of protection among member countries is fifty years.

The *C.A.* 1956, *s.* 23, gives power for the extension of such provisions to any other country, provided that "Her Majesty is satisfied that . . . provision has been or will be made under the laws of that country whereby adequate protection will be given to owners of copyright under this Act".

The symbol © is internationally recognised as denoting a copyright work.

PROGRESS TEST 15

1. What is the purpose of the law of copyright ? **(1)**

2. What is the meaning of "qualified person" for the purposes of the law of copyright ? **(3)**

3. For how long does copyright last ? **(5, 6, 7, 23)**

4. Define "literary work". **(8)**

5. Must a copyright work be one of literary or artistic merit ? **(9, 21)**

6. "Ideas" are not "literary or artistic work"—explain. **(10, 25)**

7. What is the element of originality necessary to establish a copyright ? **(11)**

8. "There is no copyright in (*a*) news, (*b*) a title, (*c*) a nom de plume." Is this right ? **(12, 13, 18)**

9. What is meant by "fair dealing" when reviewing a book ? **(17)**

10. Mr. and Mrs. Jones commission Flash, a professional photographer, to produce a photographic portrait of both of them to commemorate their silver wedding. Soon afterwards, they both die in an air disaster. Flash, still possessing the negatives, wishes to sell them to a national newspaper. Advise him. **(30)**

11. Can an assignment of copyright be made by word of mouth ? **(33)**

12. What was the purpose of the international conventions held at Berne in 1885 and subsequently ? **(36)**

CHAPTER XVI

OFFICIAL SECRETS

1. Explanation. Official secrets are protected by the *Official Secrets Acts* 1911, 1920 and 1939. These statutes are construed as one (*O.S.A.* 1911, *s.* 2(1)).

SECTION ONE

2. Spying: O.S.A. 1911, s. 1. This section, as amended, provides:

"(1) If any person for any purpose prejudicial to the interests of the State (*a*) approaches, inspects, passes over, or is in the neighbourhood of, or enters any prohibited place . . . or (*b*) makes any sketch, plan, model or note which is calculated to be, or might be, or is intended to be, directly or indirectly useful to an enemy, or (*c*) obtains, collects, records or publishes or communicates to any other person any secret official code word or pass word, or any sketch, plan, model, article or note, or other document or information which . . . might be or is intended to be directly or indirectly useful to an enemy, he shall be guilty of an offence.

"(2) On a prosecution under this section it shall not be necessary to show that the accused person was guilty of any particular act tending to show a purpose prejudicial to the safety or interests of the State, and . . . he may be convicted if, from the circumstances of the case, or his conduct, or his known character as proved, it appears that his purpose was a purpose prejudicial to the safety or interests of the State; and if any sketch, [etc.] . . . relating to or used in any prohibited place . . . or anything in such a place, or any secret official code word or pass word, is made, obtained, collected, recorded, published or communicated by any person other than a person acting under lawful authority, it shall be deemed to have been made, obtained, collected, recorded, published or communicated for a purpose prejudicial to the safety or interests of the State unless the contrary is proved."

NOTE: what is a "purpose prejudicial" is a matter for the Crown's exclusive jurisdiction—*Chandler* v. *D.P.P.* (1964).

3. Meaning of "prohibited place". The *O.S.A.* 1911, *s.* 3, as amended by the 1st Sch. to the *O.S.A.* 1920:

"(*a*) any work of defence, arsenal, naval or air force establishment or station, factory, dockyard, mine, minefield, camp, ship or aircraft belonging to or occupied by or on behalf of [Her] Majesty, or any telegraph, telephone, wireless or signal station, or office so belonging or occupied, and any place belonging to and occupied by or on behalf of [Her] Majesty and used for the purpose of building, repairing, making or storing any munitions of war, or any sketches [etc.] . . . relating thereto, or for the purpose of getting any metals, oil or minerals of use in time of war;

(*b*) any place not belonging to [Her] Majesty where any munitions of war, or any sketches [etc.] . . . relating thereto, are made, repaired, gotten or stored under contract with, or with any person on behalf of, [Her] Majesty;

"(*c*) any place belonging to or used for the purposes of [Her] Majesty which is for the time being declared by order of a Secretary of State to be a prohibited place for the purposes of this section on the ground that information with respect thereto, or damage thereto, would be useful to an enemy; and

"(*d*) any railway, road, way or channel, or other means of communication by land or water (including any works or structures being part thereof or connected therewith) or any place used for gas, water, electricity works or other works of a public character, or any place where munitions of war, or any sketches [etc.] . . . relating thereto are being made, repaired or stored otherwise than on behalf of [Her] Majesty, which is for the time being declared by order of a Secretary of State to be a prohibited place for the purposes of this section, on the ground that information with respect thereto, or the destruction or obstruction thereof, would be useful to an enemy."

4. Incitement. It is also an offence to solicit, incite or endeavour to persuade a person to commit an offence under the *Official Secrets Acts* (*O.S.A.* 1920, *s.* 7).

SECTION TWO

5. The "catch-all" Section 2. Journalists have for years sought the repeal of the *O.S.A.* 1911, *s.* 2, because it can embrace matters unconnected with national security and be used as a form of censorship. It provides:

"(1) If any person having in his possession or control any secret official code word or pass word, or any sketch, plan, model, article, note, document or information which relates to or is used in any prohibited place, or anything in such a place, or which has been made or obtained in contravention of this Act, or which has been entrusted in confidence to him by any person holding office under [Her] Majesty, or which he has obtained or to which he has had access owing to his position as a person who holds or has held a contract made on behalf of [Her] Majesty, or as a person who is or has been employed under a person who holds or has held such an office or contract, (a) communicates the code word [etc.] . . . to any person other than a person to whom he is authorised to communicate it, or a person to whom it is in the interests of the State to communicate it; or (b) retains the sketch [etc.] . . . in his possession or control when he has no right to retain it, or fails to comply with all directions issued by lawful authority with regard to the retention or disposal thereof; or (c) fails to take reasonable care of, or so conducts himself as to endanger the safety of, the sketch [etc.] . . . that person shall be guilty of [an offence].

"(2) If any person receives any official . . . document or information, knowing, or having reasonable ground to believe, at the time when he receives it, that the . . . document or information is communicated to him in contravention of this Act, he shall be guilty of an offence unless he proves that the communication to him of the . . . document or information was contrary to his desire."

6. Section 2 not confined to secrets. In 1948, after a journalist had been fined for obtaining information from a Post Office telephonist, the Attorney-General said in the Commons that he did not agree that the Official Secrets Acts were restricted to cases of spying, but promised not to "invoke grand considerations of national security merely to punish actions which some official might find inconvenient".

7. Applications of s. 2. Despite the Attorney-General's assurance, subsequent administrations have seen the use of *s.* 2 over trivial matters with no aspect of national security. Sir Lionel Heald once said in a letter to *The Times* (20th March 1970) that *s.* 2 would cover even the number of cups of tea served in a Ministry office.

A Post Office clerk was warned that he was in breach of the *O.S.A.* 1911, *s.* 2 by writing to the *Redbridge Guardian* a letter complaining of under-staffing at his post office.

In 1956 the *Empire News* published the memoirs of Albert

Pierrepoint, the public hangman. The editor was warned that if he published any matters revealed to Pierrepoint in the course of his official duties, he and Pierrepoint would be liable to prosecution under *s*. 2.

In 1932, a Fleet Street reporter and a Principal Probate Registry clerk were jailed for publishing information about wills of three public men only a few hours before the information was publicly available from Somerset House.

In 1972, Colonel "Sammy" Lohan, former secretary of the D Notice Committee, wished to review, in *The Spectator*, Greville Wynne's book *The Man from Moscow*. The Ministry of Defence considered it would be "inappropriate". The Colonel was later reported as saying: "I don't see why I should disclose anything in reviewing a book. I would have merely commented on the book as a book."

In 1974 publishers were "persuaded" by police not to publish the memoirs of a former Drugs Squad officer because, among other things, there would be a contravention of *s*. 2. The publishers were not satisfied that this was so, but felt, according to press reports, that "if passages were detrimental to the police, we should not publish".

In 1973 Harold Evans, editor of *The Sunday Times*, was threatened with prosecution under *s*. 2 for publishing a story about projected cuts in railway services (*see* XI, **9**).

8. The Sunday Telegraph case. In 1970 the *Sunday Telegraph* published "An appreciation of the Nigerian conflict", based on a report by the defence adviser to the British High Commission in Lagos, which found its way via a colonel to freelance journalist Jonathan Aitken. The disclosure led to proceedings under *s*. 2 against the Colonel, Mr. Aitken, the newspaper, and its editor, Brian Roberts.

They were all acquitted after a summing-up in which Mr. Justice Caulfield said the Crown admitted that the report bore "not a word affecting our national security".

He went on: "We all recognise that the opinion-forming and informing media like the press must not be muzzled. The warning bark, you may think, is necessary to help in maintaining a free society. If the press is the watchdog of freedom and its fangs are drawn, all that will ensue is a whimper, possibly a whining, but no bite."

The judge ventured the view: "This case, if it does no more, may well alert those who govern us at least to consider, if they have time, whether or not *s.* 2 of this Act has reached retirement age and should be pensioned off."

9. The "pensioning off"—the Franks Committee. The *Sunday Telegraph* case led to the setting up of the Franks Committee, "to carry out a full review of the operation of *s.* 2 of the *O.S.A.* 1911".

The Committee reported in 1972, recommending the replacement of *s.* 2 by a more limited statute which would cover the passing of official information relating to Cabinet decisions, defence and other secrets. A further three years passed before the Queen's Speech of 1975 stated:

"Proposals will be prepared to amend the Official Secrets Acts and to liberalise the practice relating to official information."

But early optimism in Fleet Street about the nature of any amending legislation—arising from meetings of an all-party Select Committee—later gave way to scepticism (*see* e.g., Peter Hennessey in *The Times*, 25th October 1976).

PROGRESS TEST 16

1. Why do journalists dislike *s.* 2 of the *Official Secrets Act* 1911 ? **(5, 6, 7)**

2. What did the Franks Committee recommend in relation to *s.* 2, and what steps, if any, are being taken to implement the recommendation ? **(9)**

CHAPTER XVII

D NOTICES

1. Explanation. A D notice ("D" for "defence") is a confidential letter issued by the Defence, Press and Broadcasting Committee informing editors that publication of a certain piece of information, regarded by the Ministry of Defence as a secret of importance, would be contrary to the national interest.

Colonel "Sammy" Lohan (*see* 4) said in 1963, in evidence in *Attorney-General* v. *Clough*, that a D notice in effect requested editors: "Please do not publish unless you take advice."

In 1967, twenty-two D notices were in operation, the last of them issued in 1964. D notices were introduced after World War II, though the Committee existed previously.

2. Disregard of a D notice. A D notice is only a request. Disregard of it is not, *per se*, an offence, though in some cases it could amount to an offence under the *Official Secrets Acts*. Disregard of a D notice could result in withdrawal by the Defence Ministry of facilities for a defence correspondent (or, if he is foreign, a deportation order).

In 1974, journalists in Suffolk complained that police officers, on orders from "a man in plain clothes", confiscated a photographer's film and searched his equipment after he had—allegedly in breach of a D notice—photographed an Army bomb squad at work. The picture did not contravene a D notice, and contravention of a D notice would consist in any event of publishing the picture, not merely taking it.

3. Basis of trust. The system operates on "a basis of trust between Press and government"—Lord Dundee, July 22, 1963.

Vice-Admiral Sir Norman Denning, who succeeded Col. Lohan as secretary of the D.P.B. Committee, agreed when giving evidence in the *Sunday Telegraph* secrets case (*see* XVI, 8) that the decision to publish rested with a newspaper editor. "In my position as secretary I can only advise him."

In a letter to *The Times* in 1973 (August 10th) the Committee's vice-chairman, Mr. Windsor Clarke, said an editor could fly in the face of a D notice and publish in defiance of it. Refuting a suggestion that the D.P.B. Committee had ordered a cut in a television programme, he said it has "no authority to order anyone to do anything".

4. The "cable vetting" affair. Colonel Lohan was secretary of the D.P.B. Committee in 1967 when he was approached by Chapman Pincher, defence correspondent of the *Daily Express*. Pincher had a story that outgoing cables were being vetted by the security authorities.

Colonel Lohan agreed with Pincher that only two D notices could possibly be relevant to this story, and neither was in fact applicable. He did, however, request the *Daily Express* not to publish. The *Daily Express* published.

Mr. Wilson, then Prime Minister, claimed that there had been a breach of two D notices. A Privy Council Committee was set up under Lord Radcliffe to investigate. When it reported in June 1967, the Committee felt unable to say that there had been a breach, and found no evidence that the editorial decision to publish the article was taken with a deliberate intention of evading or defying D notice procedure or conventions.

In its annual report for 1968, the Press Council said the Radcliffe Committee had acquitted the *Daily Express* on all counts. Lord Devlin, Press Council chairman, commented: "There are too many people ready to prefer an official accusation to a newspaper denial. Had it not been for very exceptional procedure, the case might have passed into currency as another example of Press irresponsibility."

5. D notices are confidential. The Radcliffe Committee also considered the action of the editor of *The Spectator* in publishing the content of the D notices. The Committee accepted that he did so under the misapprehension that his paper was not a participant in the D notice system. "We think the only safe rule, if there is to be a D notice system at all, is that all notices be treated as confidential documents, guarded with care under editorial control, and withheld from publication."

6. D notices as face-savers. The D.P.B. Committee consists of representatives of all the Services and the media. This Press and broadcasting representation on the Committee helps to allay journalists' fears that D notices may be used to spare civil servants' and ministers' embarrassment rather than to protect national security. But the suspicion still lurks.

Andrew Wilson, *The Observer* defence correspondent, wrote (26th February 1967): "From time to time, a correspondent must ask whether the system is being used to cover up facts which in his opinion the public should know . . . ."

But he added: "It is generally very difficult to know with complete certainty what constitutes a genuine security consideration; while 'the duty to tell the public' can too easily be confused with the urge to get a good story regardless of the consequences."

In 1967, the *Daily Express* (*see* **7**) said there must be suspicion whether the D notice system was "being used and extended, not to maintain the security of the State, but to suit the convenience of the government".

7. Challenge by Daily Express. In 1967 the *Daily Express* published the names of men said to be the heads of Britain's security services, contrary, so it was said, to a D notice. The names had already appeared in a newly published book which was being serialised in an American magazine, and the newspaper said it would be asking too much to expect the British public to believe that their security would be threatened by the publication in British newspapers of a report, true or false, of which the rest of the world was already aware. (A D notice "dies" in any event when its subject matter is published; *see* **8**.)

And Mr. Marcus Lipton M.P. pointed out that "every foreign ambassador in London knows who the head of the secret service is from the moment of his appointment".

8. Termination of a D notice. D notices are kept under review, and are rescinded when they become obselete. They are automatically rescinded when their subject matter has appeared in print.

PROGRESS TEST 17

1. Is it an offence to disregard a D notice ? **(2)**

2. "The D notice system operates on trust"—explain. **(3)**

3. What did the Radcliffe Committee decide in the "cable vetting" affair ? **(4)**

4. Are D notices themselves confidential ? **(5)**

5. Describe the constitution of the Defence, Press and Broadcasting Committee. **(6)**

6. Are D notices used as government face-savers ? **(6)**

7. When does a D notice expire ? **(8)**

CHAPTER XVIII

INCITEMENT

1. Incitement to racial discrimination. The *Race Relations Act* 1965, *s.* 6(1), provides:

"A person shall be guilty of an offence . . . if, with intent to stir up hatred against any section of the public in Great Britain distinguished by colour, race or ethnic or national origins . . . he publishes or distributes written matter which is threatening, abusive or insulting . . . being matter or words likely to stir up hatred against that section on grounds of colour, race, or ethnic or national origins."

Section 2 provides that "publish" and "distribute" mean publish or distribute to the public at large or to any section of the public not consisting exclusively of members of an association of which the person publishing or distributing is a member; "written matter" includes any writing, sign, or visible representation.

Prosecution requires the consent of the Attorney-General.

In *Race Relations Board* v. *Applin* (1974) two men who distributed literature aimed at inducing foster parents in their area not to take in coloured children were held to have incited them to do an act (i.e. discriminate on grounds of race, etc., when providing services to the public or a section of the public) made unlawful by the *Race Relations Act* 1968. (Section 12 of the 1968 Act provides that a person who deliberately incites another to do an act made unlawful by that Act shall be treated as doing the act.)

NOTE: The *Race Relations Act* passed by Parliament in 1976 has now made it an offence to publish a report, even if fair and accurate, of, e.g., a speech or an event, if the report is likely to foment racial hatred. Fair and accurate reports of court or Parliamentary proceedings are excluded.

2. Incitement to disaffection. The *Incitement to Disaffection Act* 1934, *s.* 1, provides:

"If any person maliciously and advisedly endeavours to seduce any member of [Her] Majesty's forces from his duty or allegiance to [Her] Majesty, he shall be guilty of an offence under this Act."

Section 2, as amended, makes it an offence for any person, with intent to commit, or aid and abet, an offence under *s.* 1, to have in his possession or control "any document of such a nature that the dissemination of copies thereof among members of [Her] Majesty's forces would constitute such an offence".

Search warrants may be issued in respect of persons and premises. The occupier must be supplied with a list of documents or other objects removed, which may then be retained for up to a month and, if proceedings are commenced within that time, until the proceedings are concluded. Prosecution requires the consent of the D.P.P.

A woman was convicted under this Act for distributing leaflets telling soldiers how to avoid service in Northern Ireland, the Court of Appeal holding that "maliciously" in *s.* 1 means "wilfully and intentionally" (*R.* v. *Arrowsmith* (1974)).

In another "Northern Ireland" case (ending in acquittals) prosecuting counsel said: "Anybody in this country is perfectly entitled to have his own political views, and to campaign for them. But what is prohibited is a political campaign . . . which actually tries to get soldiers to defect, or to make them disloyal to their oaths of allegiance" (*The Times* 11th December 1975).

It is an offence to incite a member of the armed services to mutiny (*Incitement to Mutiny Act* 1797), or to seek to cause disaffection among members of a police force (*Police Act* 1964, *s.* 53(1)).

3. Incitement to break a contract. It is a tort at common law to induce a person, without lawful excuse, to break his contract with a third party (*Lumley* v. *Gye* (1853)). A succession of legislation since 1906 culminated in the *Trade Union and Labour Relations Act* 1974, *s.* 13 of which gives immunity in tort to an act consisting of a threat that a contract of employment (whether or not the maker of the threat is a party to the contract) will be broken. However, procuring breaches of an employer's commercial contracts outside a trade dispute may still be tortious (*Stratford* v. *Lindley* (1965)).

For other forms of incitement, *see* XVI, **4** and XXII, **5**.

PROGRESS TEST 18

1. What is the offence under *s.* 6(1) of the *Race Relations Act* 1965? **(1)**

2. Explain the decision in *Race Relations Board* v. *Applin* (1974). **(1)**

3. Explain the conviction of Pat Arrowsmith under the *Incitement to Disaffection Act* 1934. **(2)**

CHAPTER XIX

REPORTERS AND OFFICIAL DOCUMENTS

1. Explanation. Apart from the requirements on public bodies (*see* VIII) to supply the press with copies of minutes and other documents, the rights of the press to see, or receive copies of, public documents, are basically those of the public. Generally, therefore, journalists' access to official documents before they are available to the public, or to documents not available to the public, depends on good will. Official reports (e.g. Command Papers) or official announcements (e.g. the New Year Honours) are generally released in advance to the press under embargo—but do not have to be.

COURT DOCUMENTS

2. No right to see court documents. A report of court proceedings which omits the name, age, occupation and address of the central figure (except where identification of that person is prohibited) is of little use. Further, it could be libellous if it identifies the accused only by name (as, e.g., in *Newstead* v. *London Express Newspapers* (1940)) and the accused has a namesake—or if the name has been taken down orally, without checking against documents, and is mis-spelt so as to be that of another person (spellings of names can vary infinitely). But reporters' right of admission to courts does not expressly include a right to see court documents such as charge sheets, indictments, pleadings, summonses, notices of motion, divorce petitions, etc. (Many of these documents do not in any event include all the material information—e.g. the accused's age, address and occupation do not appear in an indictment.)

Lord Widgery must have contemplated that pleadings in the High Court be not available to the press when he said in a Practice Note in 1973, requiring the inclusion of plaintiffs' ages in pleadings: "This need not result in additional publicity being given to the plaintiff's age, and indeed may well have the opposite effect, since it will often make it unnecessary for the judge to call for this information in open court."

3. "Give addresses in open court". No privilege attaches to anything in court documents which is not stated in open court (*R.* v. *Astor* (1913)); *Harper* v. *Provincial Newspapers* (1937)—*see* II, **14**). In 1968, a Home Office circular reminded magistrates' clerks of the desirability of giving addresses in open court, so as to make them part of the "proceedings", and thus give reports the protection of privilege. Such protection applies, however, only to "fair and accurate" reports, and the accuracy with which this information is taken down can be ensured only by checking against court documents.

4. Obstacles by officials. Official measures have sometimes rendered difficult the access by reporters to the documents mentioned in **2**, or denuded such documents of the requisite information. Some officials have said that allowing reporters to see such documents contravenes the *Official Secrets Act* 1911, *s.* 2. In view of the section's wide ambit (*see* XVI, **5**) they are no doubt right, but the promised abolition of *s.* 2 may dispose of this objection.

NOTE: when an accused person is committed for trial, notice of this fact must be posted at the courthouse (*Criminal Justice Act* 1967, *s.* 4).

When mechanical recording replaced many of the shorthand writers in the High Court, officials produced a form for the entering of names and addresses of parties and witnesses in the Family Division, "for the use of the Mechanical Recording Department and for no other purpose". The forms replaced those previously in use, which contained no such restrictive words.

A Practice Direction issued in 1975 by the Senior Registrar with the concurrence of the Lord Chancellor directed that, where a registrar permits the omission of a petitioner's name from a divorce, etc., petition (under powers in the *Matrimonial Causes Rules* 1973, *r.* 9(1)) "care shall be taken that the effect of the order is not nullified by information included in other documents".

5. Obstacles by statute. The *Rehabilitation of Offenders Act* 1974, *s.* 9, (*see* X, **20**) presents problems for court officials in relation to documents containing references to "spent" convictions. Handing such a document to a reporter would render the official (and no doubt the reporter) liable to prosecution.

6. Inspection of writs. Writs and orders in the High Court may be inspected (Order 63, *r.* 4, *Rules of the Supreme Court*). So, too, may a county court register of judgments (*County Courts Act* 1959, *s.* 101).

SOME OTHER PUBLIC DOCUMENTS

7. "Agonies". Indices of births, deaths and marriages may be inspected (*Births and Deaths Registration Act* 1953, *s.* 30). Notices of marriage announcements may be inspected in register offices (*Marriage Act* 1949, *s.* 64(2)) and at the General Register Office (*s.* 65). In both cases a fee may be charged.

In 1950 an official direction purported to prohibit reporters and others from taking notes of marriage announcements "for commercial purposes or for publication in the press". After the measure had been denounced as "bureaucratic nonsense" and had been the subject of questions in Parliament, it was rescinded so far as it concerned the press.

8. Wills. Wills, when published at Somerset House, are available for public inspection (*Supreme Court of Judicature Act* 1925, *s.* 171). A fee may be charged. But *see* XVI, **7**, for a case where disclosure was made prematurely.

9. Companies register. The Register of Companies, both public and private, is open to inspection at Companies House (*Companies Act* 1948, *s.* 462). The Register of Business Names may also be inspected (*Registration of Business Names Act* 1916, *s.* 16). A fee may be charged.

10. Bankrupts' register. This may be inspected, but not if the registrar is dissatisfied with the reason (in which case appeal lies to the High Court) (*Bankruptcy Rules* 1952, *r.* 360). A fee may be charged.

In *Re Poulson, a bankrupt* (1976) Granada Television Ltd. were refused leave to inspect a transcript of evidence given by Mr. Reginald Maudling in a private examination in Poulson's bankruptcy. (Mr. Maudling had issued a writ for libel against Granada.)

11. Registered trading agreements. These may be inspected (*Restrictive Trade Practices Act* 1956, *s.* 11(4)). A fee may by charged.

12. Town planning documents. A local planning authority's structure plan must be available for public inspection not later than its submission to the Secretary of State (*Town and Country Planning Act* 1971, *s.* 8(2)). A similar provision, after approval of the structure plan, applies to local plans (*s.* 12(2)), and to planning applications (*s.* 34(3)). Schemes under the *Community Land Act* 1975 must, as soon as possible after they have been made or revised, be open to public inspection, and copies must be available for a reasonable sum (Sch. 5 to the 1975 Act).

Local authorities' statements of case before planning appeals may also be inspected (*Inquiries Procedure Rules* 1969, *r.* 6(5)).

13. Other council documents. (*See* VIII, **5**). In 1976 a council was fined for failing to produce account documents to an elector during the week preceding District Audit. The decision was later under appeal.

14. Local ombudsman. Reports of a Local Commissioner for Administration are open to public inspection, and their availability must be announced by public notice (*Local Government Act* 1974, *s.* 30).

PROGRESS TEST 19

1. Can a reporter demand to see court documents ? **(2)**

2. How may the *Rehabilitation of Offenders Act* 1974 impede, if at all, the inspection of some court documents by reporters ? **(5)**

3. Explain the public's right to inspect (*a*) an index of birth registrations at Somerset House; (*b*) a published will; (*c*) a company registration. **(7, 8, 9)**

CHAPTER XX

ELECTIONS

1. False statements about election candidates. The *Representation of the People Act*, 1949, *s.* 91(1), provides:

"Any person who ... shall, for the purpose of affecting the return of any candidate at an election, make or publish any false statement of fact as to the personal character or conduct of the candidate, shall be guilty of an illegal practice, unless he can show that he had reasonable grounds for believing, and did believe, the statement to be true."

2. Injunctions. A person publishing a false statement as described in **1** "may be restrained by interim or perpetual injunction of the High Court or a county court from any repetition ... and ... prima facie proof of the falsity of the statement shall be sufficient" (*R.P.A.* 1949, *s.* 91(2)). An appeal lies to the High Court from a county court decision.

In *Burns* v. *Associated Newspapers Ltd.* (1925) the court refused an injunction to restrain a newspaper from describing Labour election candidates as "communists".

3. Elections—libel. No privilege attaches to a statement in an election address (*Defamation Act* 1952, *s.* 10), nor to any reports of such statements.

4. Elections—expenses. The *R.P.A.* 1949, *s.* 63, provides that no expenses shall be incurred "with a view to procuring the election of a candidate at a Parliamentary or local government election except with the permission of the candidate or his agent", and that expenses incurred must be shown by the candidate as election expenses. It provides, however, that publication of a candidate's views, the nature or extent of his backing, or the disparagement of a candidate, shall not infringe the section if "in a newspaper or other periodical".

Section 95 prohibits the publication or distribution of literature or posters not bearing the printer's and publisher's name and address, for the purpose of procuring a candidate's election.

In *R.* v. *Tronoh Mines Ltd.* (1952) a newspaper advertisement shortly before a general election condemned Labour Party policies. The judge held that *s.* 63 was concerned with expenditure on advertisements supporting a candidate in a particular constituency, not those supporting a party's interests generally.

In *D.P.P.* v. *Luft* (1976) the House of Lords held that the distribution of literature urging electors not to vote for National Front candidates in three constituencies where they were standing infringed *s.* 63 because incurring expenditure for the purpose of opposing candidate A was (especially in a constituency where, as was not the case here, there was a straight fight) tantamount to incurring it for the promotion of candidate B. (There was also an infringement of *s.* 95—*see* above).

In 1965 a Scottish court held that Sir Alec Douglas-Home did not need to make a return of expenditure on party political broadcasts on television because the broadcasts were to give information to the public, and not to promote Sir Alec's election (*Grieve* v. *Douglas-Home* (1965)).

5. Reporters' admission to election counts. Reporters have no statutory right to attend election counts. Replying to an inquiry by the N.U.J. in 1975, the Home Office stated: ". . . as the first duty of the returning officer is to conduct the election efficiently in accordance with the law, it must be left to his discretion who, apart from those entitled to be present, may be admitted to observe the count".

Where journalists do attend, they must make a declaration of secrecy.

PROGRESS TEST 20

1. Explain the offence of publishing a false statement about a election candidate. Is any defence available ? **(1)**

2. What remedy is open to an election candidate about whom a false statement is published ? **(2)**

3. What is the offence under the *Representation of the People Act 1949, s.* 63 ? **(4)**

4. Have reporters any legal right of admission to election counts ? **(5)**

CHAPTER XXI

NEWSPAPER COMPETITIONS AND ADVICE COLUMNS

COMPETITIONS

1. "Spot the Ball". The House of Lords decided in *News of the World Ltd.* v. *Friend* (1973) that a "Spot the Ball" competition run by the newspaper did not infringe *s.* 47(1)(*a*) of the *Betting, Gaming and Lotteries Act* 1963, which reads:

'It shall be unlawful to conduct, in or through any newspaper, or in connection with any trade or business or the sale of any article to the public—(*a*) any competition in which prizes are offered for the forecasts of the result either—(*i*) of a future event; or (*ii*) of a past event the result of which is not yet ascertained or not yet generally known . . ."

The competition winner was the entrant whose cross was closest to the spot where the ball ought logically to be in the opinion of a panel of experts—not necessarily the true position. In this, the organiser had been "ingenious" said Lord Hailsham. For an offence under that paragraph there must be, he said, a forecast, an event, and a result. If all these three elements were present, there would be an offence, no matter what the degree of skill involved in the forecast; but if one or more were lacking—as here, through the organiser's ingenuity—the competition escaped *s.* 47(1) (*a*).

2. Lotteries. Lord Hailsham warned, however, that a competition which escaped *s.* 47(1) (*a*) might offend under *s.* 47(1) (*b*), which makes unlawful "any other competition success in which does not depend to a substantial degree upon the exercise of a skill", and *s.* 41, which provides that "subject to the provisions of this Act, all lotteries are unlawful". He left that question undecided.

In *Blyth* v. *Hulton & Co. Ltd.* (1908) a competition in which entrants were required to complete the last line of a limerick and pay a 6*d* entry fee was held to be a "lottery". But in *Readers'*

Digest Association Ltd. v. *Williams* (1976) it was held that there is no "lottery" where a competitor is not required to make any payment.

3. Competitions involving skill. Where the degree of skill is substantial, these are not unlawful (*see s.* 47 (1) (*b*) in **2**). Thus a picture puzzle (to which more than one solution was possible, but which had no pre-determined solution, and which required considerable skill) escaped (*Witty* v. *World Service* (1936)); but an easy crossword puzzle, with many possible solutions, may not (*Coles* v. *Odhams Press Ltd.* (1936)).

4. Withholding of prizes. In a 1976 adjudication, the Press Council said that where a newspaper does not award a prize in, e.g., a literary competition, because in its view none of the entries deserves it, the newspaper should say so, either in the rules, or subsequently.

ADVICE COLUMNS

5. The Hedley Byrne doctrine. A newspaper which offers its readers advice (e.g. financial, legal) may, if it gives negligent advice, be liable under the doctrine in *Hedley Byrne & Co. Ltd.* v. *Heller & Partners Ltd.* (1963) whereby in some circumstances damages may be awarded for pecuniary loss through negligent advice.

6. Exclusion of liability. The insertion of a clause purporting to exempt the newspaper from liability in respect of any advice should generally be effective, but probably not in a case of gross negligence (e.g. where no effort is made to check the advice).

7. The Pearson case. In *De la Bère* v. *Pearson* (1908) a newspaper invited readers to seek its investment advice. A reader seeking the name of a good stockbroker was given that of an undischarged bankrupt, and lost heavily. Although there was at that time no liability in negligence for such loss, the court held that, as the newspaper had acquired the benefit of publishing the reader's letter and thereby stimulating reader interest, the reader had given value for the advice and could thus succeed against the newspaper *in contract*.

PROGRESS TEST 21

1. What, according to Lord Hailsham, was the "ingenuity" of the organiser of the *News of the World* "Spot the Ball" competition ? **(1)**

2. What are the three essential ingredients of an offence under the *Betting, Gaming and Lotteries Act* 1963, *s.* 47(1) (a) ? **(1)**

3. Could a "Spot the Ball" competition be unlawful as a lottery ? **(2)**

4. Explain the *Hedley Byrne* doctrine. **(5)**

5. Can a newspaper effectively exempt itself from liability for bad advice ? **(6)**

6. What was decided in *De la Bère* v. *Pearson* ? **(7)**

CHAPTER XXII

ILLEGAL ADVERTISEMENTS

GENERAL

1. Explanation. The editor and publisher of a newspaper are responsible for everything, including advertisements, published in the paper. Certain types of advertisement are illegal. Not only may their publication give rise to prosecution, but it will make the payment for the advertisement irrecoverable as being an illegal consideration (*Smith's Advertising Agency* v. *Leeds Laboratory Co.* (1910)). Furthermore, libel may subsist in an advertisement, and it has been held that malice by an advertiser will 'infect" the publisher (*Smith* v. *Streatfeild* (1913)) though this decision is now doubtful in view of *Egger* v. *Viscount Chelmsford* (1964)—*see* II, **26**.

2. Defences. In some instances statute provides that there shall be no offence by the publisher where he publishes innocently: words to the effect that the publisher received the advertisement in the ordinary course of his business, and did not know of, and had no reason to suspect, circumstances whereby its publication would infringe the Act in question.

3. Advertisements for return of stolen property. It is an offence (*Theft Act* 1968, *s.* 23) to print or publish an advertisement offering a reward for the return of stolen goods if it uses "words to the effect that no questions will be asked, or that the person producing the goods will be safe from apprehension or inquiry, or that any money paid for the purchase of the goods, or advanced by way of loan on them, will be repaid".

4. Sex discrimination. By the *Sex Discrimination Act* 1975, *s.* 38, it is an offence to print or publish an advertisement which might be understood to indicate an intention to discriminate on grounds of sex in employment—e.g. "waitress", "postman"— or in the provision of education, goods, or services, except in a private household or a business employing fewer than six persons, or in the circumstances where discrimination is not unlawful under the Act.

5. Incitement. In *Invicta Plastics Ltd.* v. *Clare* (1975) it was held to be unlawful to advertise a device for detecting police speed traps, this being an incitement to infringe the *Wireless Telegraphy Act* 1949.

MEDICAL

6. Diseases. The *Pharmacy and Medicines Act* 1941, *s.* 8, makes it an offence to publish any advertisement referring to any articles in terms calculated to lead to their use for treating Bright's disease, cataract, diabetes, epilepsy or fits, glaucoma, locomotor ataxy, paralysis or tuberculosis.

It does not apply to advertisements by local authorities, governing bodies of voluntary hospitals, or any person acting under authority of the Secretary of State.

It is a defence to show that the advertisement was published only so far as reasonably necessary to bring it to the notice of members of either House of Parliament, a local authority, a hospital governing body, doctors, nurses, pharmacists, authorised sellers of poisons, student doctors, nurses or pharmacists, and persons who sell or supply surgical appliances.

The *Medicines Act* 1968, *s.* 93, makes it an offence to issue a false or misleading advertisement of any medical product. Whether or not the advertisement accurately describes the composition of the product, it is misleading if it falsely describes the product itself, or is likely to mislead as to its nature, quality, uses or effects.

7. Venereal diseases. The *Venereal Diseases Act* 1917, *s.* 2, provides:

"A person shall not by any advertisement ... offer to treat any person for venereal disease, or offer to prescribe any remedy therefor, or offer to give, or give, any advice in connection with the treatment thereof."

8. Cancer cures. Under the *Cancer Act* 1939, *s.* 4, makes unlawful advertisements offering to treat, or prescribe any remedy for, cancer, or referring to any article(s) in terms which are calculated to lead to the use of such articles for the treatment of cancer.

The same defences apply as in **6**, above. Additionally, a defence of innocent publication applies. Prosecution requires the consent of the Attorney-General or the Solicitor-General.

9. Abortion. It is illegal (*Pharmacy and Medicines Act* 1941, *s.* 9) to advertise any article in terms calculated to lead to its use in procuring a miscarriage. Prosecution requires the consent of the Attorney-General or the Solicitor-General.

CHILDREN

10. Adoption. Under the *Adoption Act* 1976, *s.* 68, it is an offence to publish an advertisement (*a*) offering a child for adoption, or (*b*) seeking to adopt a child, or (*c*) stating that a person other than an adoption agency is willing to make adoption arrangements.

The *Adoption Act* 1958 included "local authorities" in paragraph (*c*), but these words are omitted from the 1976 Act. Thus where a television programme features children who are awaiting adoption and invites would-be adopters to "phone in", the co-operation of the local authority in making the programme is, it is submitted, no longer in itself sufficient, and one would need to make clear that adoption may be arranged only through an adoption agency.

11. Child care. The *Children Act* 1958, *s.* 37(1) requires that an advertisement offering to undertake, or arrange for, the care and maintenance of a child, must truly state the advertiser's name and address.

GAMBLING

12. Gaming. The *Gaming Act* 1968, *s.* 42, prohibits advertisements informing the public of premises where gaming takes place, or is to take place, or inviting the public to participate, or to subscribe money or money's worth to be used in gaming (whether in this country or abroad), unless it is for the use of gaming machines at, e.g. bazaars, sporting events, etc.; or is for use at entertainments not held for private gain, or for gaming at a travelling showman's pleasure fair. (This list is not exhaustive—see the Act for further details.)

A defence of innocent publication is available.

The provisions do not apply (*s.* 42(2) (*c*)) to

> "the publication in any newspaper of a notice stating that a licence under this Act has been granted, if the notice is published not later than fourteen days from the date on which the licence was granted, or from such later date as may be appointed by the licensing authority by whom the licence was granted, and the licence is in a form approved by the licensing authority".

13. Betting offices. The *Betting, Gaming and Lotteries Act* 1963, *s.*10(5), forbids any advertisement indicating that premises are a licensed betting office, or where such premises may be found, or drawing attention to their facilities. A defence of innocent publication is available.

14. Lotteries. The 1963 Act also prohibits the publication, or possession for publication, of any advertisement of a lottery. It is a defence to prove that it was a small lottery incidental to some entertainment, or for charitable or sporting purposes, or in accordance with the *Art Unions Act* 1846.

> NOTE: the *Lotteries Act* 1975 gives the Secretary of State power to make regulations governing the advertisement of lotteries.

BUSINESS

15. Consumer Credit Act 1974. Under *s.* 45 it is an offence to advertise oneself as willing to provide credit under, e.g., a hire purchase agreement if the supplier is not holding himself as willing to supply the goods or services for cash; or if the advertisement is false or misleading (*s.* 46). The publisher also commits an offence (*s.* 47) but has a defence of innocent publication.

The provisions also apply to an advertisement indicating willingness, in the course of a business, to advise on debts, and effect transactions for their liquidation; but not if the advertiser indicates that he is not willing to act in relation to consumer agreements (*s.* 151). A defence of innocent publication is available.

The Secretary of State has power to make regulations governing advertisements for consumer credit business.

16. Fair Trading Act 1973. Section 23 prohibits advertisements which contravene any "consumer trade practice" Order made under the Act. A defence of innocent publication is available.

17. Trade Descriptions Act 1973. Section 3 (dealing with trade descriptions in advertisements relating to a given class of goods) makes it an offence if all goods of that class do not comply with the description. A defence of innocent publication is available.

18. Hallmarking Act 1973. This Act forbids advertisements containing misleading descriptions relating to gold, silver or platinum. A defence of innocent publication is available.

19. Protection of Depositors Act 1963. It is an offence (*s*. 1) to induce another person, by the reckless making (dishonestly or otherwise) of any statement, promise or forecast which is misleading, false or deceptive (*a*) to invest money on deposit with the advertiser or any other person, or (*b*) to enter into any agreement for that purpose.

Section 2 provides that no person shall issue an advertisement inviting the public to deposit money with him, except for specified trustee investments, or deposits with a banking or discount company, building society, friendly society, or industrial and provident society.

20. Insurance Companies Act 1964. Section 62 prohibits advertisements inviting persons to take out insurance unless regulations made by the Secretary of State are complied with.

21. Moneylenders Act 1927. Moneylending advertisements are unlawful (*s*. 4) if they contain particulars other than: the moneylender's business name, business address, any former business address, present telegraphic address and telephone number; a statement that he lends money with or without security; the highest and lowest sums he is prepared to lend; and the date when his business was first established.

22. Trading Stamps Act 1964. Section 6 makes it an offence to convey in an advertisement for a trading stamp scheme the value stated on a trading stamp by means of a statement associating the worth of such stamps with what the holder pays to obtain them, or in misleading or deceptive terms.

MISCELLANEOUS

23. Plant Varieties and Seeds Act 1964. Advertising the seed of a new plant variety before such seed has been subjected to performance trials, and the results published, is an offence (*s.* 22(4)).

24. Advertisements for sex. *See Shaw* v. *D.P.P.* (XII, **17**) (conspiracy to corrupt public morals by publishing a directory of prostitutes) and *Knuller* v. *D.P.P.* (XII, **17**) (advertisements for homosexuals). In *Knuller*, it was suggested that advertisements for heterosexual partners would also be unlawful.

25. Cruelty to Animals Act 1876. It is an offence to advertise exhibitions of experiments on living animals calculated to give pain.

26. Houses to let. The *Accommodation Agencies Act* 1953, *s.* 1(1) (*c*), prohibits advertisements describing any house as being to let without the authority of the owner or his agent.

27. Racial discrimination. Advertisements indicating intent to discriminate on racial grounds in the provision of, e.g., goods, services, housing or employment, are illegal. *Race Relations Act* 1968, *s.* 6).

28. "Telling Stork from butter". In *Van den Berghs & Jurgens Ltd.* v. *Independent Broadcasting Authority* (1976) a judge held that a television advertisement comparing Stork margarine with butter contravened the *Margarine Regulations* 1967. The Regulations also apply to other forms of advertisement.

PROGRESS TEST 22

1. Give examples of some types of illegal advertisements. **(3–28),**
2. Explain what is meant by a defence of "innocent publication and give examples of advertisements to which this applies. **(2)**

CHAPTER XXIII

THE PRESS COUNCIL

1. Explanation. The Press Council, established in 1953, exists to defend individuals against unfair treatment by the press, and the press against unfair attacks by the government and other power structures.

2. Defending the public. The Press Council hears complaints of unfair treatment by the press (e.g. hounding, or publishing an inaccurate story and refusing to publish a correction or explanatory letter). If it finds the complaint established, it will censure the newspaper concerned, and by agreement a newspaper will publish the Press Council's critical adjudication against it. A complainant is required to undertake not to pursue any other remedy.

3. Defending the press. The Press Council makes its voice heard when press freedom is under attack by, e.g., proposed legislation. It submitted evidence to the Royal Commission on the Press in 1975, the Faulks Committee on defamation, the Phillimore Committee on contempt, the Franks Committee on official secrets, and the Younger Committee on privacy. It defended the *Daily Express*'s stand against Mr. Wilson's criticisms over the "cable vetting" affair (*see* XVII, 4).

4. Press esteem for the Council. The Press Council has not always enjoyed the unanimous support of the press. John Gordon once wrote in the *Sunday Express*, when a reader threatened to report him to the Press Council: "You can report me to Madame Tussauds, the Society for the Protection of Sputniks, NATO, UNESCO. . . ."
But the Younger Committee found that the Council is today "respected, feared and obeyed".

5. Criticisms of the Council. Two typical criticisms have come from Parliamentarians: "the only sanction against editors is condemnation, and condemnation in such an inoffensive manner"; "the Council is inadequate as a watchdog of both press and public".

6. The Council's answers. Lord Pearce, then Press Council chairman, said in 1973: "To be compelled to print in your own newspaper an account of a matter which shows that in the view of a fair and sensible jury you were hitting below the belt or acting in a manner unworthy of your profession is a strong sanction."

The Council was charged with maintaining press freedom—the "linchpin of democracy"—and preventing abuses of this freedom, because these could lead to its loss by providing an excuse for controls.

7. Declaration of Principle. In 1966 the Council negotiated a Declaration of Principle, intended as an affirmation of a principle accepted by the whole of the press. The principal provision is:

"No payment should be made for feature articles to persons engaged in crime or other notorious misbehaviour, where the public interest does not warrant it."

8. Composition of the Council. The Council consists of a lay chairman (an eminent lawyer—two have been former Law Lords), representatives of, e.g., the Guild of British Newspaper Editors, proprietors' organisations, the N.U.J., the I.O.J., and some laymen.

9. Younger Committee recommendations. The Younger Committee recommended that lay members should form one half of the Council's membership. It also recommended that critical adjudications should, if possible, receive similar prominence to the original article.

PROGRESS TEST 23

1. What are the functions of the Press Council ? **(1, 2, 3)**
2. Do you think the Press Council is an adequate watchdog for both public and press ? **(5, 6)**
3. What was the effect of the Press Council's Declaration of Principle in 1966 ? **(7)**
4. Describe the constitution of the Press Council (*a*) today, (*b*) as recommended by the Younger Committee. **(8, 9)**

THE ENGLISH LEGAL SYSTEM

SOURCES OF LAW

1. Statute. Acts of Parliament (or "statutes") are—subject only to E.E.C. Regulations or Directives in the fields in which they operate—the supreme and unassailable source of law. This applies whether the statute is a public or private Act (*Pickin* v. *British Railways Board* (1974)). A public Act is of general application; a private Act applies only to a particular locality or undertaking.

2. Statutory instruments. A statute often empowers a specified person (e.g. a government Minister) to make rules, regulations or orders. Any rules, etc., which are so made will have the force of law if they are properly laid before Parliament and if they are within the authority conferred by the statute. If they are outside that authority, they may be declared *ultra vires* ("beyond the Minister's powers") and therefore void.

3. Judicial precedent. Most of our law is embodied in reports of cases which have been decided over the centuries. A decision of the House of Lords, Court of Appeal, or a High Court judge, sets a precedent which inferior courts are bound to follow, whether they like it or not, in subsequent cases based on similar facts. A High Court judge is not bound to adhere to a decision of one of his brother judges, and the House of Lords (since 1966) is not bound by its own previous decisions. The Court of Appeal (Civil Division—*see* **7**) is, however, generally bound by its own previous decisions (*Young* v. *Bristol Aeroplane Co.* (1944)). The Judicial Committee of the Privy Council (*see* **6**) in theory is not bound by precedent and does not create precedent. As, however, its personnel are mostly the same Law Lords who sit judicially in the House of Lords, its decisions carry great persuasive weight.

The part of the decision which creates the precedent is called the *ratio decidendi,* or "reason for deciding". In the course of a judgment a judge may make *obiter dicta* ("incidental observations") which, though not creating binding precedents, provide useful pointers.

PROCEEDINGS

4. Civil and criminal proceedings. A civil wrong is one committed against another person or persons, but not against the Queen's peace (e.g. a breach of contract, or a tort such as negligence, trespass or defamation). The remedy is an action by the injured party for damages, or possibly an injunction against repetition—or both.

A crime is a wrong against the Queen's peace, the remedy for which is a criminal proceeding in which the accused may, if convicted, suffer a sanction at the instance of the State.

Civil proceedings are to compensate (though in rare cases punitive damages may be awarded). Criminal proceedings are to punish and reform, and to deter others (though criminal courts have some powers to order a convicted person to compensate his victim).

Magistrates courts have both criminal and civil jurisdiction.

COURTS AND THEIR PERSONNEL

5. The House of Lords. The Appellate Committee constitutes the highest court in the land, and consists of Lords of Appeal in Ordinary (peers who have held high judicial office). It hears appeals from the Court of Appeal (both Divisions), and from co-ordinate courts in Scotland and Northern Ireland. Appeals may be brought in civil and (except from Scotland) in criminal matters, but only if leave is granted either by the inferior court or by the Appeal Committee of the House. Leave will be granted only if the case involves a point of law of general public importance. The *Administration of Justice Act* 1969 enables certain appeals to go direct from the High Court to the House of Lords.

6. Judicial Committee of the Privy Council. This Committee, consisting of Lords of Appeal in Ordinary and some Commonwealth judges, hears appeals from certain Commonwealth countries and Protectorates, etc. It also hears appeals on ecclesiastical questions, and from some disciplinary bodies such as the General Medical Council.

7. The Court of Appeal. This has a Civil Division and a Criminal Division.

In the Civil Division three (sometimes two) Lords Justices of Appeal hear appeals from the High Court, the county courts, the Restrictive Practices Court, and some tribunals.

In the Criminal Division three Lords Justices of Appeal (or, more frequently, a Lord Justice of Appeal and two judges of the Queen's Bench Division) hear appeals against conviction and/or sentence by persons convicted in the Crown Court.

8. The High Court. This consists of three Divisions:

(a) *The Queen's Bench Division:* hears actions in contract and tort, and also includes the Admiralty Court (collisions at sea, salvage, and "prize" disputes) and the Commercial Court (certain specialised commercial disputes).

A Divisional Court of the Queen's Bench Division hears appeals on points of law from magistrates' courts and certain tribunals. It will also quash the decision of *any* inferior court or tribunal if it has been reached in breach of the rules of natural justice (e.g. if a party has not had a fair opportunity of being heard) and it will command a person, who has failed to carry out a public duty imposed on him by statute, to do so.

(b) *Chancery Division:* its jurisdiction includes such matters as disputes over land, mortgages, trust funds, probate, wills and intestacies, partnerships and companies, trade marks and copyrights, patents, and appeals over income tax. It frequently grants such relief as injunctions, orders for specific performance, rectification of documents, etc.

Two judges of this Division sitting together hear appeals and applications in bankruptcy matters.

(c) *Family Division:* This Division hears contested matrimonial causes (e.g. for divorce, nullity of marriage, judicial separation); ancillary matters such as financial provision; and adoption, legitimacy, guardianship and wardship of minors.

Two judges of this Division sitting together hear appeals from domestic proceedings in magistrates' courts, including adoption, guardianship, affiliation, etc.

NOTE: Judges of the High Court nowadays generally sit alone. Juries sit only in such cases as defamation, false imprisonment and malicious prosecution, in the Queen's Bench Division.

9. The Restrictive Practices Court. This consists of a High Court judge as chairman, assisted by four experts in industry and commerce. It decides whether certain trading agreements can be justified under the *Restrictive Trade Practices Act* 1956 or the *Resale Prices Act* 1964. Appeal lies, on points of law, to the Court of Appeal (Civil Division).

10. The Crown Court. A major court (e.g. Winchester) is presided over by a High Court judge. It generally tries the more serious cases, and *must* try any class 1 offence, e.g. murder, offences carrying the death penalty, *Official Secrets Acts* offences (*Courts Act* 1971). Lesser offences (e.g. burglary) may be tried before courts of a lower "tier"—e.g. those presided over by a Recorder. Where the accused pleads not guilty, a Crown Court trial is before a jury. The counts against an accused person are set out in an "indictment" (pronounced "inditement") and an offence which is triable before the Crown Court is said to be "indictable".

The Crown Court also hears appeals on criminal matters from magistrates' courts. For this purpose a jury does not sit.

11. County courts. Their jurisdiction, subject to certain financial limits, includes actions in contract and tort, disputes over trusts, mortgages, land, company windings up, adoption and guardianship of minors, and actions under the hire purchase and rent restriction legislation, and under the *Race Relations Act* 1968 and the *Sex Discrimination Act* 1975. Some county courts also have jurisdiction in bankruptcies and undefended divorces. Appeals lie to the Court of Appeal (Civil Division).

A county court is presided over by a county court judge. Small cases (or, by consent, any case) may be tried by a registrar.

12. Coroner's courts. A coroner inquires into the cause of any death where this does not immediately appear to have been from natural causes, particularly where the death was violent or unnatural. In some cases (e.g. road or rail accidents) a jury must be empanelled. Coroners also inquire into treasure trove (i.e. coins, bullion, etc., found buried, where ownership is unascertained).

13. Magistrates courts. Most magistrates courts are staffed by unpaid, and usually unqualified (though they do nowadays undergo training) Justices of the Peace appointed by the Lord Chancellor, and assisted by a legally qualified clerk. In stipendiary magistrates' courts, in some of the larger cities, a legally qualified magistrate sits alone.

Their criminal jurisdiction consists of hearing summary cases (e.g. the less serious motoring offences), hybrid offences (which may be tried either before magistrates or before the Crown Court), and certain indictable offences (*see* **10**) which can be tried before magistrates. Appeal against a decision of a magistrates' court lies to the Crown Court, or, in some instances (on points of law only) to a Divisional Court of the Queen's Bench Division (*see* **8**)

Magistrates also sit as examining justices to decide whether a sufficiently strong case has been made out against a person charged with an indictable offence to warrant his committal for trial before the Crown Court For this purpose a lay magistrate may sit alone.

A specially selected panel of magistrates sits as the juvenile court, hearing proceedings—other than homicide—against persons aged from ten to seventeen, or in respect of persons under seventeen.

Magistrates' civil jurisdiction consists of domestic proceedings (matrimonial disputes, but not divorce, between spouses; affiliation orders; adoption, etc.). Appeal lies to the Family Division of the High Court (*see* **8**).

Magistrates also sit as licensing authorities, hearing applications for liquor, betting office, etc., licences. These proceedings are administrative, not judicial.

14. Administrative tribunals. These tend to deal with a variety of questions, often of a specialised nature—e.g. the amount of compensation payable for compulsorily purchased land, whether an employee has been unfairly dismissed, whether a claimant is entitled to social security, etc. Some tribunals (e.g. the Lands Tribunal) have a legally qualified chairman assisted by professionally qualified laymen. Others are staffed entirely by laymen. Appeals lie from the superior tribunals (e.g. the Lands Tribunal) direct to the Court of Appeal (Civil Division). Other tribunals have differing appeal procedures (e.g. in National Insurance cases appeal lies to the National Insurance Commissioner, and in some cases to the Secretary of State).

REPORTED CASES

Some readers may wish to read fully the reports of some of the cases cited in this book. To assist them (assuming that they have access to a law library) a table of cases has been included.

Numerous series of law reports existed until the establishment of the modern system of law reporting in 1865. An example is the Meeson & Welsby series of reports. The reference (or, rather, *a* reference) for *Parmiter* v. *Coupland* is (1840) 6 M. & W. 105. This means that the report is to be found in the sixth volume of Meeson & Welsby's Reports at page 105. The year is shown in round brackets to indicate the antiquity of the case!

Where, however, the year is an essential part of the reference (as it is in most of the modern series of law reports) it is shown in square brackets. Thus *Cassidy* v. *Daily Mirror Newspapers Ltd.*, reported at [1929] 2 K.B. 331, is to be found in the second volume of the King's Bench Reports for 1929, at page 331. Without knowing the year one cannot find the appropriate volume.

The modern series of law reports most commonly cited are: A.C. (Appeal cases: House of Lords and Judicial Committee of the Privy Council); Ch. (Chancery Division: cases in that Division, and appeals therefrom to the Court of Appeal); Q.B. (Queen's Bench Division, and appeals); Fam. (Family Division, and appeals); P. (the former Probate, Divorce and Admiralty Division, and appeals therefrom); and the W.L.R. (Weekly Law Reports) and All E.R. (All England Reports) which include cases from all the above courts.

APPENDIX III

BIBLIOGRAPHY

Sir Robert McEwen & Philip Lewis, *Gatley on Libel and Slander*, 7th edn. (Sweet & Maxwell, 1974)

P. F. Carter-Ruck, *Libel and Slander*, 3rd edn. (Faber & Faber, 1972)

Professors Borrie & Lowe, *The Law of Contempt* (Butterworth, 1973)

C. J. Miller, *Contempt of Court* (Elek, 1976)

Sir David Lidderdale, *Erskine May: Parliamentary Practice*, 19th edn. (Butterworth, 1976)

Professor Harry Street, *Freedom, the Individual and the Law*, 3rd edn. (Penguin, 1972)

C. T. Latham & John Richman, *Stone's Justices' Manual*, 108th edn. (Shaw & Sons and Butterworth, 1976)

G. L. Simons, *Pornography without Prejudice* (Abelard-Schuman, 1972)

D. Madgwick & A. Smythe, *The Invasion of Privacy* (Pitman, 1974)

E. P. Skone James, *Copinger and Skone James on The Law of Copyright*, 11th edn. (Sweet & Maxwell, 1971)

Command Papers (H.M.S.O.):

Radcliffe Committee on D Notices (1967)	Cmnd. 3312
Salmon Committee on Tribunals of Inquiry (1969)	Cmnd. 4078
Younger Committee on Privacy (1972)	Cmnd. 5012
Franks Committee on Official Secrets (1972)	Cmnd. 5104
Phillimore Committee on Contempt (1974)	Cmnd. 5794
Faulks Committee on Defamation (1975)	Cmnd. 5909

Law Commission Working Papers 54, 57, 58, 62, 63, 75 (H.M.S.O.)

EXAMINATION TECHNIQUE

1. Read the rubric carefully. It is idiotic to "throw" an examination through answering too few or too many questions, or too few or too many questions from one part of the paper.

2. Read the questions carefully. It is no less idiotic to throw away all or most of the marks on a question through not reading the question with sufficient care. You will get no marks —and, indeed, may lose marks—for irrelevance.

At the start of the examination read the question paper carefully from beginning to end. Jot down beside the questions any points you would wish to make, and any principles of law, statutes, cases, etc., which appear to be relevant. In a three-hour paper, you should spend at least twenty minutes reading the question paper and planning your answers (*see* **4**). The candidate who starts his first answer almost as soon as he sits down is usually destined for failure.

Having read the question paper, decide which questions you like most (or dislike the least!)—the questions which you are best equipped to answer. It may be that certain statutes, cases, etc., are at the back of your mind, but you cannot instantly remember their names. Here lies one advantage of reading the entire question paper at the outset; it may well be that, as the examination progresses, they will come to you. But don't worry if they don't; principles are the things that matter. It is much more important that you know that restrictions apply (unless waived) to the reporting of committal proceedings, than that you know that these restrictions are imposed by *s*. 3 of the *Criminal Justice Act* 1967. You are being examined as a student of journalism, printing or publishing, not as a law student.

Do not worry if, at first, you feel unable to answer the requisite number of questions. The author's experience is that in the course of writing your first answers you get inspiration, and perhaps unearth material, which will help in your last answer. Very often your most "doubtful" question produces your best answer.

3. Ration your time. Each question carries a maximum number of marks—and seldom does any candidate score a maximum on a question. It is better to "half-answer" the requisite number of questions than to fully answer half that number.

4. Plan your answers. Having selected your questions and made your jottings beside them, draw up a brief plan of each answer (a reasonable proficiency in shorthand, which any trainee journalist should have, is a distinct advantage here). This plan will enable you to develop your answers step by step, and show lucidity of thought—a characteristic essential to journalists and lawyers alike.

5. Textbook questions. Example:

"It is possible effectively to poison the fountain of justice before it begins to flow"—discuss.

Here you would consider the strict view taken by some judges, especially in Scotland (and their decisions are judicially respected in England) of the meaning of "pending or imminent" proceedings. It would obviously be germane to refer to the case of *R.* v. *Parke* (1903) where Mr. Justice Wills spoke the words quoted in the question (story held to be a contempt although proceedings were not "pending" at the time of publication) and the decisions in *R.* v. *Evening Standard Co. ex parte D.P.P.* (1924) and *R.* v. *Beaverbrook Newspapers Ltd.* (1962) (*see* VI, **12**). Of course, you would not forget *s.* 11 of the *Administration of Justice Act* 1960 (*see* VI, **6**). So far as civil proceedings are concerned, the advice given by Lord Reid in *Attorney-General* v. *Times Newspapers Ltd.* (1974) (*see* VI, **15**), and the decision in *Re F, a minor* (*see* VI, **17**) should obviously be discussed.

6. Problem questions. Example:

The editor of the *Duckswood Diatribe* has received an irate letter from Frederick Wainwright, who was convicted last month in the local magistrates court of committing indecent assault upon a girl aged fifteen, and placed on probation for two years. The newspaper reported the conviction as being one of a "serious offence against a young girl" and omitted to quote the words of the chairman of the Bench: "We accept that here was a promiscuous girl who told you she was eighteen, and looked every day of it, and that she made all the running". Wainwright threatens to sue for libel. Discuss.

When answering this type of question, it is a good idea to start off by stating the rule (you are set for some marks if you at least show the examiner that you know this). Thus, set out the effect of *s.* 3 of the *Law of Libel Amendment Act* 1888 (*see* II, **11**) that absolute privilege applies to a fair accurate and contemporaneous report, in a newspaper, of judicial proceedings heard in public. These were judicial proceedings heard in public, and the report was in a newspaper, so it remains to consider whether the report was fair, accurate and contemporaneous.

(*a*) *Fair?* A report which omits to set out matters in favour of a party—which matters would, if reported, give the case an "entirely different complexion"—is not "fair" (*Wright & Greig* v. *Outram & Co.* (1890)). But it is questionable whether the failure to report the chairman's observation renders this report unbalanced to that degree.

(*b*) *Accurate?* The charge(s) need not be set out in full; a fair summary will suffice. But whether or not the charge was "serious" was not a matter for the newspaper to adjudicate upon (cf. X, **3**); indeed, the chairman's remark, and the probation order, suggest that the Bench took a somewhat different view. The word "young" gives the impression that the girl was rather more than a few months below the age of consent. (Cf. cases such as *Mitchell* v. *Hirst, Kidd & Rennie* (1936)—*see* II, **12**) where the privilege has been lost through inaccuracy.

(*c*) *Contemporaneous?* We are told that Wainwright was convicted "last month", but not when the report was published or how frequently the paper appears. If the report was published say, three weeks after the conviction, and the newspaper appears weekly, it is doubtful whether the report would be "contemporaneous". It certainly would not be if the newspaper appears daily.

Should it be held that the privilege is lost, there remains the defence of justification. Section 13 of the *Civil Evidence Act* 1968 (*see* II, **7**) establishes, for the purpose of a defamation action, that Wainwright committed the offence of which he was convicted, and if the court takes the view that his reputation is not materially injured by the words not proved to be true, his action will fail (*Defamation Act* 1952, *s.* 5: *see* II, 9).

> NOTE: Do not be afraid that the examiner may disagree with your view. There is always room for more than one view, otherwise there would never be any litigation—and judges' decisions would never be reversed on appeal. You will score marks by showing that you understand the principles and, based upon them, have argued your case cogently. Try to see arguments for and against, and then give your reasons for preferring one to the other.

INDEX

Details of some other Macdonald & Evans
publications on related subjects can be found
on the following pages.

For a full list of titles and prices write for the
FREE Macdonald & Evans Business Studies
catalogue and/or complete M & E Handbook
list, available from Department L3,
Macdonald & Evans Ltd., Estover Road,
Plymouth PL6 7PZ

Advertisement Writing
FRANK JEFKINS

Written by an author who has had many years of experience as a copywriter, this book provides an exhaustive and colourful analysis of the techniques and influence of copywriting. It also incoporates many examples — taken from British and foreign advertising campaigns, past and contemporary — which clearly illustrate both the positive impact as well as the shortcomings of different copy-writing styles.

Illustrated

Basic French
ARNOLD KELLETT

This HANDBOOK sets out the fundamentals of the language, emphasising the kind of French needed for "O" Level and C.S.E., but it is also intended as a concise revision course for "A" Level or similar examinations. In addition, since it takes nothing for granted, it is a useful practical guide for adults who are starting French from scratch.

Illustrated

British and American Business Terms
RUDOLF SACHS

This book should prove invaluable to all those engaged in banking, exporting, importing and insurance, to students of economics, and to the general reader interested in modern international commerce.

"The scope of this slim volume is considerably wider than its title implies. It provides concise descriptions of the principal sectors of the economy and the most important economic institutions in Great Britain and the United States, arranged alphabetically under 138 key terms." *Business Administration*

Business Typewriting
SYLVIA F. PARKS

This HANDBOOK sets out the theory of typewriting layout and is intended as a revision book for examination candidates or as a convenient work of reference for the office typist. It contains notes on the arrangement of many forms of typewritten matter, with diagrams and examples, and covers the typewriting examination syllabuses of the R.S.A., the C.S.E., Pitman's and other examining bodies.

Illustrated

English for Professional Examinations
J. R. L. McINTYRE

This HANDBOOK — previously entitled *Intermediate English* — has been retitled to reflect the wide range of readers for whom the new edition caters. Students of professional intermediate examinations and those taking "O" and "A" Level English will find guidance on how to approach the most recent style of questions, many of which are included.

General Principles of English Law
P. W. D. REDMOND

Originally designed for those preparing for intermediate professional examinations, this HANDBOOK has also proved itself immensely popular with "A" Level and university students. The latest edition includes the facts of appropriate recent cases and several important new topics.

Guide to the Social Services
FAMILY WELFARE ASSOCIATION

Published annually to be as up to date as possible this invaluable guide gives comprehensive cover of the various services, both statutory and voluntary, which are available to the community, and data as full as possible concerning the wide field of legislative procedure. There are also sections giving an extensive range of information to assist social workers and students.

Income Tax
HENRY TOCH

Intended for students in accountancy, law, secretarial practice and business studies, this HANDBOOK explains in concise form the basic principles of income tax law and practice.

Modern Lithography
IAN FAUX

Beginning with the key scientific aspects of printing and ending with a discussion of different litho inks and papers, this book provides a widely ranging coverage of modern lithography for students of printing. Special features are the helpful glossary of printing terms, and chapters on photo-lithographic platemaking and planning. ". . . Offers a great deal of valuable help to beginners as well as experienced lithographers." *Small Printer*
Illustrated

Modern Business Correspondence
L. GARTSIDE

Designed for all who write, dictate or type business letters, this extensively-revised new edition covers all aspects of the subject from the essential grammatical background to composition, style, display and typing. Related topics discussed in some detail include business reports, telecommunications, filing and office-machine systems.

Illustrated

Model Business Letters
L. GARTSIDE

Over 500 specimen letters, indexed for quick reference, deal with almost any business situation likely to arise, with a commentary outlining the commercial and legal relationships each one creates. Other features are the glossaries of terms and classified lists of expressions useful when composing letters.